Out of the Shadows

An Exploration of Dark Paganism and Magick

John J. Coughlin

Revised second printed edition published by
Waning Moon Publications, LLC
Post Office Box 79
Cold Spring, NY 10516
USA
waningmoonpublications.com

ISBN-13: 978-0-9823549-7-1
ISBN-10: 0-9823549-7-5

2nd revised edition

Ankh-pentacle design by Nicole Graf, 2000.

To Write to the Author

If you wish to contact the author, or would like more information about this book or future publications, please write the author at the below mailbox. Both the author and the publisher appreciate hearing from you and learning of your enjoyment of this book and how it has helped you. The author cannot guarantee that every letter can be answered, but all will be read. Please write to:

John J. Coughlin
PO Box 79
Cold Spring, NY 10516

Please enclose a self-addressed, stamped envelope for reply
or $1.00 to cover costs.
If outside the U.S.A., enclose an international postal reply coupon.

For an email and social media visit:

http://www.JohnCoughlin.com

Visit *Out of the Shadow*'s web site, "An Exploration of Dark Paganism," as well as other projects of the author at:

http://www.waningmoon.com

To Hecate, who taught a frightened little boy not to be afraid of the dark...

Winter

Autumn winds are dying
As winter rears its head.
Soon the land will sleep again
In the silence of the dead.

The gray sky seems a blanket.
The golden trees now bare;
Their branches reach out to the sky
To grasp the misty air.

Dark browns replace the orange
And grays replace the blue
Soon snow will change this landscape
As the spiral dance holds true.

The silence will be welcomed
By a solitary crow.
An eerie song of mystery
That few will ever know.

For winter keeps its secrets,
The ones not hard to hide.
The answer's all around us,
But the question sleeps inside.

-John J. Coughlin, November 24, 1999

In loving memory of Botanica.
My familiar. My friend.

Into your dark embrace, oh Hecate,
do I entrust my companion
until we can one day be together
in the realm between eternity and the now.

ꟼꞀₘ𐌗LUꟲꜝꞂ ꟲₘꟲₙ ꟱ₙUꟘLU꟱Ꞁ ꞡꞀ𐌗Ꞁꟲₙ 𐌗Ꝗ ꟭Uꞡ꟱ₙꝆ

Table of Contents

Introduction to Second Edition

It has been over 15 years since I first released *Out of the Shadows*, and the world has changed on so many levels. This was a world before the iPod (let alone iPhone and iPad), 9-11, or a black US President. The idea of legalized gay marriage in any US state was still just a dream, and Myspace and Facebook (and social media in general) were at best still just ideas on paper. It staggers my mind to think of how these alone have reshaped the world and how we interact with it.

I can't take credit or blame for any of these, but I am humbled by some of the influences this book had when it first came (excuse the pun but I can't resist) out of the shadows. Back then the idea of Dark Paganism was not openly discussed in fear of being misunderstood by the white-light mentality that was so prevalent at the time. I had, in fact, expected backlash when the book was finally in print, but to my surprise the bulk of the responses were in the form of a thank you. I had given a name and voice to feelings and ideas that many others shared or were wrestling with. I challenged ideas some were clinging to because they did not understand that they did not have to confirm for the sake of conformity. Forums dedicated to the subject formed (since social media was not yet a thing), and budding new authors who would eventually carry the torch contacted me to share ideas and seek encouragement. I was eventually considered by some the "Father of Dark Paganism." As this darker take on Paganism began to become more trendy, other publishers began to seek out authors to tap that emerging market. I was asked more and more for another book, and approached often to consider forming a tradition or organization around my ideas.

And then, at a time when I could have ridden this wave and claimed some level of authority on the subject, I fell silent. The book remained in print, but not actively promoted, and my public appearances became few and far between. But why?

Well, there were two main reasons.

First, I never wanted to create a trend. Trends attract people with a superficial interest in the subject. I wrote for people who truly resonated with this vague and complex topic of darkness in spirituality. To me, this was something that was personal and required each individual to find their own understanding and place in all this. To create a tradition or organization around it, or to TELL you what to believe, went against the very nature of what I was trying to express. *Out of the Shadows* was not – and is not– an instructional manual. It is my attempt to create a sort of collage of ideas and imagery from which you can discover your own path and/or find a sense of balance in your beliefs. Quite frankly, I do not write for the masses – I write for kindred spirits – and do not seek to be a professional author focused on sales and notoriety. And so I stepped back to let the ideas ripple out for others to discover when the time was right.

Secondly, as I continued to evolve personally and spiritually, I did not want to cling to a snapshot of where I was at the time of its writing, or rest my laurels on the accolades of the past. I had to let it go in order to focus on my development and personal Initiation, and that journey has been an interesting one to say the least!

However, back in 2010 I began to entertain the idea of a revised edition so that I could share with you what I have learned and experienced since the book's release. How could I add that material while keeping to the spirit of the original work?

Over the next few years, each time I attempted a revised edition I found myself wanting to write a new book. It was not that I disagreed with what I had written; it still to this day stands on its own, outside of a few dated references to then current events perhaps. It was a snapshot of (and legacy to) the thinking of the person I was back then, who was simply not the person I was now. To revise it from my current perspective ran the risk of losing the spirit of the person who wrote it. No, if I have more to say I can entertain a companion volume.

And so, with only minor corrections and tweaks, I re-release *Out of the Shadows* to carry on the Work it started back in 2000-2001. Perhaps the re-release will serve as a new ripple of influence as those who can use the book the most discover it.

I wanted to take a moment to recognize all of you who have contacted me over the years, be it via email or social media, or during one of my workshops (when I was doing those more regularly). It was from such interactions that I furthered myself in many ways. I have always considered teaching a two-way street, and I have learned much from so many of you over the years.

John J. Coughlin
Cold Spring, NY
January 7, 2016

Introduction to First Edition

As a child I recall watching the movie *Star Wars* and thinking how much I wanted to join the "dark side." It wasn't that I wanted to be a "bad guy", but rather that the dark side was more interesting. The villains had the better outfits, better weapons, and more interesting powers. Sure they always lost in the end, but until then they really kicked ass.

As the saga continued and I matured, the characters began to gain depth and still the dark side continued to hold my fascination. If it wasn't the evil that attracted me, then what was it? Obviously there were more subtle connections being made... the dark side meant more than just the side of the villain.

The truth is, the dark side *empowered* me. Sure, a part of me yearned for power **itself**, especially during those awkward teen years when it seemed the whole world was against me. But even now, as a reasonably well-adjusted adult, the dark side draws me.

Whereas the light side is based on restraint, the dark side says to let go. It seemed to me that the dark side was not bad in itself, it was simply easier in which to become carried away. Give someone too much freedom and they either hurt themselves, or they learn to exist within certain self-defined boundaries. Many just lack the discipline and foresight to handle such freedom and need external rules to keep them in check; others refuse to allow themselves to be confined by the ideals of others.

Perhaps, when properly handled, the dark side had much to offer once we learned to steer free of its pitfalls. It also seemed to me that the universe was not easily divided into the good and the bad, the light side and the dark side.

And so my exploration of darkness informally began... thanks in part to George Lucas.

This book is a culmination of over two decades of study and practice, being a combination of many traditions as well as my own personal adaptations and insight. It is in no way intended as an introduction of a new tradition, but merely a basic guide to what I have found effective and comfortable.

The goal of this book is to not only share with you my views on Dark Paganism and spirituality, but to encourage you – if not challenge you – to personalize your own belief system. Although sometimes written in a Wiccan context, many of my views may not agree with more traditional Wiccan, or even Pagan, views.

If some of the items in this book disturb you, then you have a wonderful opportunity to explore *why* you are disturbed. This can only bring you closer to solidifying your own belief system. If you find yourself trying to defend your own beliefs, or feel threatened by what you read here, then perhaps you have found a weakness in your own system.

I am, by far, not stating that my views are necessarily the correct or best views, but they work for me and that is what matters. They are also not rigid and constantly evolve with me. My point is to show that darkness is not something to be cast away in Paganism. When modern Pagan religions such as Wicca were young, they were more balanced, recognizing the important role that *both* darkness and light played in the spiral dance called life. It is only recently, when Paganism became popular, if not trendy, that people began misinterpreting this polarity and separating them.

The second part of this book discusses the nature and practice of magic by exploring the underlying principles at work. Originally these notes were to be part of a second book, which may still one day find its way into print. Since the misconceptions of darkness and magic are interwoven, I felt that this book would be incomplete without touching on the subject of magic.

You will find no spells or rituals in this book. There are more than enough books out there to fill that need. You will, however, gain a better understanding of what is happening *behind* those spells, and hopefully, after reading this book, you will no longer have the need for those silly compendiums of empty spells. The spell is just a prop – the *real* magic occurs within.

Your criticism is most welcome. However, please read with an open mind and try to understand the reasons behind why certain things are said or done. Keep in mind that this book is an <u>exploration</u> into the many subjects of darkness and magic. I have tried to be as in-depth as possible, but each topic could easily fill a book of its own. I can only hope I have done each topic justice in such limited space.

Darkest of Blessings,
John J. Coughlin
(a.k.a. "Dark Wyccan")

Part 1

Darkness

Dark Paganism

There are some who find comfort in the shadows,
Who strive to comprehend the mysteries,
Who find solace in the silence of a winter night,
Who sing softly to the Crone.
We are the Dark Pagans, children of the Dark Mother.
                                                    -John Coughlin

So often darkness is associated with evil. Since the term evil has no place in a nature-based religion, we Pagans are forced to look beyond such stereotypes.

Evil is a human term. It begins and ends with us. A tornado is not evil, yet it is destructive. Fire can be used to benefit life or destroy it. Nature is neither good nor evil; it simply is. It follows no moral code and has no internal motive. Only humans, with our complicated set of emotions and intellect, can justify such categorizations.

Death, destruction, chaos... these are essential driving forces within nature. Life feeds on life; destruction precedes creation. These are the only true laws, and they are not open to interpretation.

When Pagans anthropomorphisize nature into something good and loving, they deny its very all-encompassing nature. When the dark deities are shunned in fear of the unknown, we deny ourselves full understanding of all deities and what they have to offer, leaving us with an incomplete picture.

It is our nature to fear the unknown. We cling to archetypal forms representing the aspects of some great unknowable, all-encompassing force, which we cannot comprehend. We call them our deities. This is not wrong; it is, in fact, necessary since we cannot easily grasp the "divine" or cosmic source otherwise.

Some religions choose to see this source as one omnipotent being. However, accepting the existence of an all-good and just being dictates that there must then exist a counterpart that encompasses evil.

Since nature-based religions view the concept of deity in a more polytheistic and/or pantheistic way, the separations of creative/destructive forces are not as well-defined. The deities take on aspects of nature or human ideals. Instead of one omnipotent being, we have deities of love, war, beauty, the sun, the moon, the sea... Each deity inherently contains both the creative and destructive forces.

It is through the many aspects of the Goddess and God that we come to learn more about the universe and ourselves. To shun those aspects we fear inhibits our growth. It is a goal of Dark Paganism to encourage those who hide behind the positive aspects of our deities to embrace their fears and learn.

As a life-affirming spirituality, Paganism often focuses on the positive, creative, and nurturing forces in nature. It is easy to lose touch with the darker aspects, particularly when we intrinsically fear them. Life begets death and death begets life. Something must always be destroyed for something to be created. Chaos is the fuel of creation.

Those who shun the darker aspects of nature and ourselves tend to fall into what I have heard called "White-Light" or "fluffy" Paganism – Pagans who think life is all happiness and joy and that once attuned to the rhythms of nature, life becomes such wonderful dreams. Many subscribers to the "New Age" movement have this shallow outlook: to them, nature is good and just and ordered.

This simply is not the case. Take these dull-eyed individuals and place them in the wilderness with nothing but their crystals and they will be some animal's dinner before the end of the week. Nature is harsh. It is unforgiving. The weak die or are killed by the strong. Life feeds on life. Even the strictest vegan is a plant killer. Humans, with their technological and medical breakthroughs, have "improved the quality life" by distancing themselves from the harshness of nature; this has softened us by removing us from nature's harsh reality.

However, despite this harsh side of nature, it is not evil. It also has its share of beauty. The point is, nature encompasses both creative and destructive forces. Ignoring the negative aspects results in an incomplete and dangerous view of nature.

It is the goal of Dark Paganism to remind us that there is a darker side to all things and that this darker side is not necessarily harmful and negative. There is beauty in darkness for those who dare enter the shadows to embrace it.

Many aspects of darkness are not as harsh as death and chaos. There is reflection, reverence, change, divination, introspection, trance, autumn[1], winter, maturity, wisdom, the distant cry of a crow in a forest, a single candle glowing in the night, the cool embrace of the autumn wind scented with the decay of leaves. These are all aspects; these are its gifts. Perhaps it is through the beauty of a sunset and sunrise and the colors of fall and spring that we are reminded of the cycles of birth-death-rebirth and of the importance – *the necessity* – of each phase.

A Need for Balance

It is important to remember that focusing only on the darker side is just as dangerous as focusing only on the lighter side. Balance is important, and even though some may relate to one aspect more than the other, we must always remain open to the other aspects. Life consists of the interplay of these opposites that naturally complement each

---

[1] Autumn and winter from the perspective of Northeastern United States; seasons of course will vary, but there is always a cycle of some form. In the autumn of my area, the leaves turn brilliant shades of orange, yellow and red, then brown, and finally fall off as the frost comes. In winter the days are significantly shorter and the wind is cold and piercing. Snow is common and there is an eerie silence in the forests.

other. To discard one aspect is to sacrifice our wholeness and limit our potential.

This balance does not necessarily (and rarely does) mean equality or neutrality. We typically have an attraction to the imagery of one side over the other. Dark Pagans have a connection to the imagery and themes of darkness, yet they do not exclude the light. Each path finds balance within itself.

Sometimes when one side becomes unbalanced, the other side attempts to compensate, but in doing so it often throws itself out of balance. I see this with many Dark Pagans who have grown so disenchanted with the "fluffy" variety of Lightside Paganism that they have begun to feel that Lightside Paganism itself is useless and lost.

In Defense of Lightside Paganism

Lightside Paganism in itself is a very viable and powerful spirituality. It may have a disposition towards the positive/nurturing aspects of nature, life, etc; but it is well-adapted in acknowledging the darker aspects as well *if allowed to*.

The problem is that fewer and fewer Pagans are obtaining any sort of formal training within a coven or grove[1] and are instead learning from very superficial "Wicca 101" books. Unfortunately, this

---

[1] Such formal training, of course, is not necessary but would then require well-developed disciplinary skills to progress. Many beginners fail to develop *any* skills since they rely solely on books and not experimentation and practice.

means that many novices from Judeo-Christian backgrounds are reading these books and interpreting them within a Judeo-Christian context. Thus, instead of grasping concepts of polarity and balance, they are too busy separating light and dark as if it is the same as good and evil. Worse, many try to over-emphasize the positive in hopes of combating the stereotype of witchcraft as evil.

There is currently a great imbalance[1] in Paganism. The overly white-light "fluffy" Pagans outweigh the truly balanced Lightside Pagans, thus the need to stress the aspects of darkness, and also why we now have a need to differentiate Lightside and Darkside Pagans.

Being a Lightside Pagan in itself is not a fault since it is simply a personal disposition, just as others have a disposition towards darker imagery. Either way, both sides recognize the existence, and the need, for the other; there is not – or at least should not be – a war between dark and light Paganism. However, as soon as one decides to *deny* darkness, then that person sacrifices wholeness.

In the same context, just because I am a Dark Pagan does not mean that I do not enjoy sitting under a tree watching the animals and birds or strolling barefoot in the grass. It simply means that my overall outlook on life, nature, and even spirituality varies from that of Lightside Paganism.

---

[1] I am pleased to say that since first releasing Out of the Shadows there has been a growing interest in and appreciation of Dark Paganism, although sometimes at they expense of it becoming trendy and thus watered down and commercialized.

Neither is more right. There is no absolute path; each must find the path that best works for them.

Since this book is primarily a reaction to the growing trend towards the unhealthy and unbalanced (also known as "fluffy") form of Lightside Paganism, sometimes it may seem to be a bit harsh towards Lightside Pagans, but then again, I do want this to serve as a wake up call.

Darksiders

Although this book is geared towards Dark Paganism and other paths of dark spirituality, themes of darkness are not just used within a religious or spiritual context. There are many non-spiritual paths and lifestyles that also fall under the category of darkness. The term *darksider* loosely addresses any individual who is naturally attracted to darkness.

Not every individual, of course, must belong to a specific dark path or lifestyle. This is key to anyone who has a leaning towards darkness; although groups of likeminded peers are always comforting, if not refreshing, the focus is not on the collective but on the individual. Each finds his or her own means of self-expression, yet through shared imagery and ideals certain communities still form, be they spiritually or aesthetically oriented.

Given the fact that the themes of darkness are rooted in archetypal imagery buried deep within our collective unconscious, it is no surprise that these individuals, although often avoiding conformity, find commonality among others in the shadows. Beyond the realm of dark spirituality lie larger groupings of individuals centered on their self-defined subcultures. Obviously, there will be a large intersection of these groups, although they are all in themselves distinctly separate.

A subculture, as defined by the Merriam-Webster dictionary, is "an ethnic, regional, economic, or social group exhibiting characteristic patterns of behavior sufficient to distinguish it from others within an embracing culture or society." The sections that follow will explore some of the more common subcultures associated with darkness.

The Gothic Subculture

Probably the most notable form of dark lifestyle or culture is the Gothic subculture. Goths, as they call themselves, are stereotypically portrayed as being depressed, pretentious, full of angst, dressing like vampires, and brooding over death and all things spooky. The stereotypical Goth is melodramatic and often wimpy, choosing to moan of their dilemmas among themselves while never standing up to those who mock them.

Indeed, to the casual observer of the gothic scene[1] many of these stereotypes may seem to hold true. The scene itself is composed of people with various

---

[1] The gothic "scene" loosely defines the people and places that make up a Goth's social environment - particularly clubs, coffeehouses, and other places they like to gather socially.

reasons for being there. Some simply enjoy the music or the erotic element, while others are full of teen angst or seek acceptance by their peers. Still others simply want to be considered cool or fashionable, while others are drawn to it because they find a deeper connection to it – a connection that cannot always be verbalized. There is not one "type" of person that associates or identifies with the Gothic scene, and thus as with most groups, the stereotypes merely exaggerate some of the more common characteristics of those most visible to the public. Typically the most visible are the worst examples and Goths themselves often enjoy making fun of these stereotypes by mocking them.

The Gothic subculture developed in the 1980s and centers around its music and fashion. It evolved in tandem with the Punk subculture, although where punks were associated with anarchy and violence, Goths were associated with angst and depression. Such feelings are indeed characteristics of these subcultures and often the impetus for initial identification with them, particularly among youth. However, these associations are typically over-emphasized by the press and those unfamiliar with these subcultures. Although not a religion, many Goths have found a comfortable amalgamation of their personal spiritualities with their lifestyles.

The term "gothic" derives from that of the gothic novel – a literary style of fiction prevalent in the late 18th and early 19th century that gave rise to such classics as Mary Shelly's Frankenstein and Bram Stoker's Dracula. These novels, like the gothic subculture, emphasize the mysterious and desolate.

Defining what makes one gothic lies not so much in taste but in self-determination. Many refuse to be considered Gothic because such categorization comes with it the typical stereotypes and expectations that any culture or group reflects. Being strongly individualistic, such people obviously prefer to avoid this labeling. However, this attitude itself is deemed "gothic", and so we are left with a reminder of the nature of darkness – it can only be analyzed so much before logic breaks down. Darkness is, after all, intuitive, and therefore explaining why certain people are drawn to it is not an easy task. Such connections are rooted in the unconscious and thus evade simple explanation.

As a culture, gothdom has developed its own protocols of behavior, and its own style of music, dance, and sense of aesthetics, which temper the individual's view of the outside. These may vary from one city to the next as each local scene carries with it its own character and style.

There is an overall distaste for, and lack of tolerance towards, those who pretend to be something they are not. One should not TRY to be gothic: instead, one should simply be themselves. One's style of dress is not intended to make one a Goth, but rather to express his or her personal style, although many are also very fashion conscious all the same.

As is common among many darksiders, black clothing and silver jewelry is predominant in their wardrobe. Many prefer to dress in renaissance or similar period styles with a flair for aristocracy. Being non-conformists, hairstyles and colors are often far from the "norm" of society. Some do this out of rebellion fueled by the pangs of teenage angst, while to others identify so completely with the subculture that these styles seem genuinely normal and attractive. The reasons vary and add to the diversity of its constituents. For some it is a phase while to others it is a lifestyle choice or calling. As to which is truly "gothic" the answer will always remain relative to the observer, for they all fall under the umbrella of what is considered the "gothic scene" for better or worse.

As with many darksiders, the use of drugs is accepted but not condoned. It is an aspect of the scene but not a defining characteristic. Being more open-minded, many Goths and similar darksiders choose to make their own decisions, sometimes based upon experimentation or casual use.

Somewhat hedonistic in nature, Goths and other darksiders are typically less bound by shame or guilt and are willing to explore these "darker" aspects of themselves. Despite this flexibility, most darksiders have learned to live within the boundaries of their physical limits and personal safety. However, some have chosen to live life on the edge and thus accept the consequences of such a lifestyle. It is not for other darksiders to judge. In fact, such individuals are often admired – not for the choice itself, but for the fact that they made the choice to live as they choose despite the dangers. They have defined their own way and regardless of how senseless it may seem even to some darksiders, they have willingly embraced all it has to offer – both good and bad. This of course is not the admiration of the addicted, for the addicted no longer make choices but rather are slaves to their addiction. There is a big difference.

Overall, the typical Goth is not self-destructive or violent. Although staunchly individualistic, they are not necessarily antisocial, albeit they prefer to keep a certain distance from people and ideals that conflict with their own.

Goths and other darksiders have a more open and accepting stance on sexuality. Because of this polyamory (the practice of having more than one committed partner), bisexuality, and various sexual fetishes are more prevalent and visible. Gender identification is more laxed and many strive for an androgynous look or style of dress.

The more serious Goths – those who are not still searching for acceptance or following the latest trend towards dark fashion – share certain characteristics along with many darksiders. Most are interested in the creative arts of some form, be it through humble appreciation or actual involvement. Musicians, artists, poets, and even talented webmasters are commonplace and often held with a certain amount of admiration or respect. Self-expression is definitely a respectable trait within the scene.

Along with this creative current comes intelligence. Most serious Goths are well read and intelligent. Often it is their intelligence that drew them to the gothic scene since the intelligent, particularly in youth, are not as readily accepted by their peers and naturally stand apart. This identification with loners is an instigating factor in association with the gothic scene for many. Most Goths share a certain sense of aloofness from the rest of the world, hence the associations with depression. Most are not constantly depressed, but have a serious side to them that tempers them towards an attitude of realism that is sometimes mistaken as or manifests as bitterness. They carry with them an aura of solemnity, which is not often appreciated until one has bypassed their defense mechanisms. Goths and other darksiders would be quick to point out that life is not fair, but rarely would they insist that life is not worth living. Instead they stress survival and making the best with what they have. This attitude is key to most darksiders and often the best defining characteristic among those who identify with darkness in general. Their often macabre sense of humor is indicative of this optimistic approach to pessimism. Goths and other darksiders are often loners and underdogs. It doesn't take much time to figure out whether someone is truly gothic at heart or simply along for the ride. Those who "just don't get it" will follow the stereotypes religiously, seeking to become something they are not.

Despite their often intimidating appearance, the typical Goth is non-violent and fights at gothic clubs and bars are far less frequent than what occurs at the more mainstream social events.

The Vampiric Subcultures

The vampire scene consists of several separate vampiric subcultures and types of vampires, each of which have their own history and dynamics. As with Goths, they carry similar stereotypes and are often mistaken as being an aspect of the gothic subculture. Indeed, there an intersection of these groups but they are far from the same. As a social scene, it is newer than the gothic scene, and its growth has been fueled by intriguing vampire stories such as Anne Rice's Vampire Chronicles, as well as the increasing availability of information through the Internet.

The stereotype of the vampire from the point of view of other darksiders is often one of contempt. They are viewed as "wannabes" who cannot accept themselves for who they are and so create something they are not. Although this does hold true within the vampire scene even more so than the gothic scene, it would be unfair to label all involved as such. Any social scene with a strong emphasis on fantasy imagery will naturally attract those wishing to escape from reality. The vampire scene, along with groups that play such fantasy games as *Dungeons and Dragons* or *Magic: The Gathering* must face this dilemma and the harsh stereotypes that follow.

Don't mistake this simple fact as sarcasm. Many can and do find a healthy connection to darkness through the imagery of the vampire mythos. All dark subcultures will attract a certain amount of "losers" and "lost souls" since they hope to find acceptance among those that seem as outcasts. By centering on a powerful mythos such as the vampire, the vampiric subcultures offer these unsavory masses an escape from reality far greater than many of the other darkside subcultures. Therefore, while all darkside subcultures must contend with a certain amount of "negative publicity" caused by such lost souls, the vampire scene tends to have more to contend with.

Of the various types of modern vampires and vampire subcultures, several broad categories can be deduced. These categories are not absolute but can assist in gaining a better understanding of the dynamics of the vampire scene. Needless to say, all constituents of the vampire scene are quite human and very few of them would refute this.

LARPers

Although not considered vampires in the literal sense, LARPers make up a large portion of the vampire scene.

LARP stands for "Live Action Role Playing." In this game, each player is given or develops a character (a vampire in this case). During the game the players are left to improvise as their character to reach specific goals laid out by the storyteller[1]. The storyteller is not a player but rather serves as a director/referee who gives the game direction by providing clues or rumors that help further the story. A LARP is also a social event where people can meet others of similar interests and build friendships. It allows for ample social interaction that clubs do not always provide.

During a LARP, a player is expected to remain in character at all cost and follow certain rules and protocols. Since LARPs often are played within the clubs and gathering places of both the Gothic and vampire scenes, players are often mistaken as being unable to separate fantasy from reality by those who are not familiar with the game. Of course, as with any role playing game, there will always be a certain number of people who prefer to hide within their self-created fantasy world. This is not the case for all LARPers, but some will always take the game more seriously than others.

---

[1] Some prefer the term "LARP Master"

Although considered here as part of the vampire scene, there is, as usual, a crossover into the gothic scene. Some Goths hold LARPers in disdain while others are avid players.

Vampire "Fanatics" and Lifestylists

The fashion and aesthetics of the 20th century vampire imagery are embraced within both the vampire and the Gothic scenes, although fangs and vampiric contact lenses are typically more popular in the Vampire scene (again this will also depend on the local scene).

Many become involved in the vampiric subculture due to their fascination with vampires. They may enjoy the stories and style so much that they wish to imitate it or make it their own. While for some this fascination is a weekend occurrence, others have chosen to incorporate it into their everyday life.

Vampire lifestylists rarely consider themselves actual vampires, but rather as merely humans with a great fascination for vampiric imagery and myth. Some create their own definitions as to what a vampire is and, apart from sometimes being accused of being somewhat elitist, do not deny their humanity and mortality. To them, a vampire is a self-actualized individual who, like other darksiders, has a special connection or calling to aspects of darkness; it is a state of mind as well as a fashion statement.

Blood Drinkers

Not all individuals in the vampire scene actually drink blood, but more in the vampire scene do so than in any other darkside scene[1]. The reason behind the drinking of blood varies greatly. Some do it out of curiosity, perhaps fueled by their fascination with vampires. Others do it simply to be "cool" or to be considered a true vampire by their peers, if not simply for the "shock value." Others seriously believe that it imparts youth and power or have a compulsion to do so.

There is also an erotic element in the drinking of the blood of another. The sharing of blood by some is a very intimate and bonding experience. It symbolizes the sharing of one's life with another more so than would the sharing of any other bodily fluid, particularly because of blood's powerful association with both life and death. This may range from a simple erotic association with blood to a form of haemotodipsia – a sexual compulsion to see, touch, and taste blood.

Blood-craving vampires have a primarily non-erotic based need or compulsion to drink blood, typically in small amounts at frequent intervals. Usually the blood is of another person. One's own blood or animal blood is rarely a viable substitute. These vampires do not claim to be immortal or possess inhuman physical strength. They do however often claim to possess a certain degree of psychic abilities and prolonged youth, but are quick to point out that such abilities do not exceed the limits of human potential.

---

[1] Goths, for example, don't typically get involved in blood drinking or blood play, but there are always exceptions.

Many genuine blood-craving vampires[1] want nothing to do with vampirism. They do not stand out in a crowd. Many become involved in the vampire scene only after their cravings begin to surface. Some do this to better find meaning behind their condition or to seek support from others of similar conditions, while others use the scene as a source for donors since they are more likely to find such willing people within the vampire scene. Most are quick to insist that this condition is far from desirable and often complicates one's life and relationships.

Although some blood-craving vampires have had a life-long fascination with blood and/or vampires, others claim to have had no such history until it was awakened within them. Such an awakening is sometimes attributed to an experience within the vampire scene while others can find no specific event or reason for the sudden craving. This awaking is often termed "turning." Some believe that the process of turning will only occur on those with a genetic predisposition to vampirism, while others simply grasp onto the condition as a psychological crutch similar to a state of codependency. Such individuals would be unaware of this predisposition until they were placed in contact with a catalyst – particularly the taste of blood. This could be analogous to someone who is predisposed to alcoholism but does not become an alcoholic until first consuming alcohol.

This concept of turning could explain the compulsive need/craving these blood drinkers describe. Whereas someone with a blood fetish

---

[1] "Genuine" as in having a true craving for blood and not doing it for shock value or to imitate vampires.

has a specific erotic element to the attraction to blood, most blood drinkers do not make that association. To them the need is a physical one resembling that of an addiction. In fact, some have described the craving as being similar to a severe nicotine fit. When this thirst is not satisfied, the inflicted often complain of physical aliments such as severe headache or nausea. Many also claim sensitivity to bright light and thus prefer the night.

Psychic Vampires

Although the specifics of the psychic vampire are often the topic of debate within the vampire community, a psychic vampire can be defined as an individual who feeds on life energy (a.k.a. "pranic" energy or chi), emotional energy, or even the sexual energy of others. This can be done consciously or unconsciously. This form of vampirism is generally considered to be potentially harmful to its victims since the draining of life energy could lead to a weakened immune system and thus running the risk of inviting illness. Victims commonly complain of fatigue or other physical discomforts after coming into contact with a psychic vampire. While blood drinkers seek willing donors, psychic vampires do not necessarily do the same.

There are two basic forms of psychic vampire: unconscious and conscious. The unconscious psychic vampire is unaware of his or her condition either due to ignorance or denial. They are usually recognized by the reactions people have to them, being viewed as demanding, clingy, or attention-seeking without any specific behavior to support this notion.

The conscious psychic vampire on the other hand, is aware of his or her condition and typically attempts to control or improve it. Like the blood-craving vampire, conscious psychic vampires have a compulsion or need to feed and can experience discomfort if ignored. Some conscious psychic vampires can also satiate their need by consuming blood, just as some blood-craving vampires can stave off their need for blood by feeding off of psychic or emotional energy. However, psychic vampires rarely have the same intense craving to feed as the typical blood-drinking vampire.

The Psychotic and Confused

The smallest grouping within the vampire scene ironically consist of those who seriously consider themselves a true non-human vampire – that they have awakened into a new level of existence. They will insist on being from another century despite their lack of historical knowledge or claim to posses great physical or psychic abilities they are unable to substantiate. Such individuals can become violent when their delusions are shattered and are not particularly welcome within the vampire community.

A term I have seen used more and more lately by younger teens – *spiritual vampire* – stands out among most other forms of self-determined vampire. People who claim to be spiritual vampires insist they are the reincarnation of a spirit or soul of a vampire. Apparently, once they become aware of their spiritual identity they are able to obtain some of their lost "powers," typically psychic powers and the ability to entrance people. Spiritual vampires claim that they must seek out their fellow vampires who have re-incarnated as their friends in order to revive an ancient coven or circle. It often ends up as a type of LARP-like game with no general direction or purpose other than eliciting a sense of belonging among their peers.

Obviously the further from reality one veers the more dangerous the delusion becomes. Using the imagery and self-association with the vampire mythos to empower oneself is relatively harmless provided the distinction between reality and fantasy remains intact. Once that distinction is lost, the threat of psychosis begins.

One of the characteristics of any darksider is a claim to the right to define oneself as one sees fit. This can be a quite liberating and empowering experience, but also dangerous for those who are easily lost in self-delusion.

Vampire Cults and Clans

Within the vampire scene occasional organized groups form. They typically will consist of vampires of similar kind (blood drinkers and their donors, psychic vampires, LARPers, vampire wannabes, etc.) Many are simple social cliques while others are more structured in their organization.

Some of these groups have developed a cult-like religion around the vampire folklore and imagery. Typically these cults are pseudo-satanic in that they borrow the imagery and aspects of Satanism and other darkside religions that fit best into their own vampiric schema. Some are legitimate Dark Pagans worshipping deities associated with vampires, such as Lilith, while others devise fictitious religions with little, if any, true spiritual intentions, often based upon popular fictional characters and stories.

There are some "cults" or "clans" that claim that the mythos of some forms of LARP derived from real vampire clans and history. Although the history is questionable, such groups do exist, but whether they are blood-craving vampires, LARPers gone astray, or borderline psychotics remains to be seen and probably varies with the group. These groups tend to be secretive, if not elitist, and so should be avoided for safety reasons unless one knows the members personally. The history behind their claims cannot be proven since it is based upon hearsay by those involved.

BDSM Subculture

BDSM refers to the various forms of bondage/dominance (or discipline) and sadism/masochism. The social scene will vary with location from bars and clubs to Internet discussion groups.

Apart from the fact that the BDSM subculture embraces and explores one's sexuality through practices of domination and submission, the subculture as a whole is not in itself easily classified as a "dark subculture", as are gothdom and vampirism. Sexual practices aside, the typical member of the BDSM subculture does not necessarily encompass the characteristics of other darksiders, nor do they typically embrace themes associated with darkness other than perhaps the equipment used during a BDSM scene[1]. Most do not wear their equipment outside of their sexual play; they are essentially "regular people" who have taken the initiative to explore their sexuality and desires and, in turn, to explore themselves. This very reason alone places them on the fringe of the darkside regardless of their appearance.

Others involved in S&M eventually find themselves drawn to dark imagery as well as their own dark nature. This form of S&M is more theatrical and highly ritualistic, being based upon a fascination with power, seduction, domination, the willing submission to pain, suffering, and humiliation. Such individuals may also become involved in the gothic or vampire scenes as they begin to explore their interest in the darkside.

Similarly, there are some darksiders that find a niche in the BDSM subculture and add to the intersection of the gothic and vampire scenes with it. These intersecting groups are typically not found at the larger BDSM events, but rather at events that share venues with Goths and/or vampires, or at events geared towards those markets. Keep in mind that, with exceptions, many in the gothic and vampire scenes utilize the regalia associated with BDSM for fashion purposes only or light experimentation and are not themselves actively involved in the BDSM subculture itself or the discipline involved. This

---

[1] Fetishists on the other hand, are considered "fellow travelers" to BDSM. Most involved in S&M are not fetishists and vice versa. Those involved in leather and rubber/latex fetishes are more likely to be involved in S&M and also involved in dark cultures such as the Gothic subculture although this is not necessarily the case.

distinction is not apparent to most in the gothic/vampire scenes for the very reason that they lack experience within the actual BDSM circuit. It is only when they venture into more established BDSM events that they realize they stand out more than expected. Those goths and vampires heavily into the BDSM scene either stick to those events designed for the combination or act and dress accordingly within each group.

It would be difficult to speak for the entire BDSM subculture when discussing its feelings towards the vampire and gothic scenes, particularly where the scenes intersect. Many maintain the attitude of "whatever works for them", while others feel such Goths and vampires who include BDSM regalia in fashion are "poseurs" for not taking an active interest in BDSM. This varied attitude is indicative of the diversity within the BDSM subculture itself.

Overall the BDSM subculture is more likely to judge based on safe practice rather than appearance, personal bias not withstanding. Each scene focuses on different aspects of one's lifestyle. As one Goth who is also involved in BDSM mentioned to me, "gothic are my ways, and BDSM are my relationships." This distinction describes how one can be involved in various scenes without conflict.

Commonalities among Darksiders

Teen angst aside, there is a natural tendency for certain people to be attracted to dark lifestyles and dark spiritual paths. There is a deeper connection that is made on the unconscious level for anyone that is drawn to the shadows. Despite their differences in approach and style, there are many underlying similarities among all darksiders that take root at the archetypal level.

These individuals share common aesthetics and an openness to explore the very things society has tabooed. Thus topics such as sexuality and drug use are no longer black and white and the individual is left with the power to make his or her own decisions. There is a general lack of violence, which has become a characteristic of those who cling to themes of darkness purely out of rebellion or mental instability. There is also a greater sense of acceptance; one's sexual preference, gender, and ethnicity are not as important as one's self-acceptance and style. Obviously, any collection of people will have its share of bad seeds, but the general consensus among all darksiders is one of acceptance, albeit there is a certain need for distance from those outside their circle.

Darksiders on the whole are intelligent and artistic or in some way creative. They maintain an overall hedonistic approach to life in that they are not afraid to enjoy themselves and entertain various fetishes or other sexual interests that the common person might hide in shame.

"Lost Souls"

The somewhat familial connection of many darkside collectives and acceptance of self-expression attracts many that desire a sense of social connection and acceptance. Social outcasts, the lonely, rebellious teens, these all find a delusional haven among darksiders. By associating themselves with a dark lifestyle or spiritual path, they become empowered by a false sense of justification and identity. Such individuals are typically teens since that is the age group that suffers from a sense of alienation and awkwardness due to puberty and the often incapacitating effects of peer pressure. However, there are also adults who never properly mature enough to develop a healthy sense of identity.

Just as many non-darksiders flock to the gothic and vampire scenes for a sense of belonging, many flock to Satanism, satanic imagery, or "witchcraft" for a sense of power which is often associated with darkness. Not finding what they had hoped from established Satanic and Wiccan teachings, these pseudo Satanists and witches develop their own form of Satanism and/or witchcraft based upon their ignorance and expectations.

Unfortunately, these pseudo-darksiders are the very ones most visible in the public eye due to their often violent or melodramatic fates. Instead of finding comfort in the shadows, they wrongly assume that an association with these dark lifestyles and spiritual paths will justify or encourage their own warped intentions.

Just as some fundamentalist Christians will temper their interpretation of the Bible to support their own biases by taking its passages out of context, pseudo-darksiders find acceptance of their own warped ideas by projecting their sickness onto anything associated with darkness.

These lost souls are not the byproduct of a dark lifestyle or spiritual path; on the contrary, they are its plague.

Darkside Survival Guide

Although the darkside subcultures mentioned in this chapter can be safe havens for those with similar interest, they are also magnets for those non-darksiders that are in search of identity, power, or sex. It is therefore important for those new to these scenes to take certain precautions.

These precautions aside, it is most important to be yourself. Self identity is the underlying factor for any darksider. Ask yourself why you wish to get involved in a certain scene. Is it a fad? To be cool? Because everyone else is in it? Are you trying to change or be something else? Are you bored? Or is there a connection there – something intangible... a drawing to it?

Legitimate darksiders will not try to make you do things you do not want to do or jeopardize your personal safety. It is simply not their way. In all my years in the gothic scene I have never been ostracized for refusing a drink or drug. Although friends may tease me for drinking hot tea more than any other beverage, they do not deem me as being less "gothic" for not making alcohol my first choice of drink. Anyone who makes you feel obligated to act a certain way is neither a friend nor a true Goth.

There is no initiation into the gothic scene. You simply go to the clubs and get to know others in the scene. There will always be pretentious individuals, but they are merely imbedded in a bubble of self-delusion. If you become overly concerned about being accepted as part of the scene then that should be a warning sign of personal misdirection. There will always be those who accept you and those who will not – their opinions, either way, should have no bearing on how you choose to define yourself. Of course, if you are a teen and coping with the pressures of that age group these words will seem foreign or over-simplified. In time, you'll either learn from your mistakes or remain a lost soul. Stay true to yourself and in the long run you will be much happier.

Remember that the vampire scene is a collection of several very different subcultures existing on many different levels, many of which do not associate with each other. When entering the scene make sure to keep aware of this and stick to those groups that fit your own personal needs and tastes. Some don't mix well and will have their own biases towards each other and themselves. Keep in mind also your reasons for wanting to get involved with this scene. Are you fascinated with vampires? Are you looking for a social scene or support group? Or do you just want to be a "real vampire"? Depending on your motivations you could simply end up the victim of another self-deluded individual. Always remain aware of what you want and be wary of what others offer. Keep clear of the delusions of others, always trusting your gut instinct.

Drinking blood or facing real dangers is not part of LARPing – when it becomes a part of the game it is no longer LARPing, it is a collection of deluded individuals. This is not do say that some blood drinkers don't LARP, but it is not an aspect of LARPing and blood drinkers keep it separate from the game. When someone starts taking the game too seriously then it is time to proceed with extreme caution.

Unlike the movies, vampires don't typically invite one to become a vampire and blood drinkers do not proselytize the advantages of doing so. In fact, most true blood-craving vampires wish they were free of their addiction and often have nothing to do with the vampire scene. If someone claming to be a vampire solicits him or her self and/or "the gift" then that should raise red flags, as should someone who claims to be a vampire includes abilities beyond the scope of human potential (super human strength, unrealistic age, etc.).

Blood drinkers thoroughly screen their donors in order to avoid infectious diseases. When they don't they are either stupid or novices. They rarely use fangs to draw blood, but rather lancets and draw very little blood at a letting. Blood drinking may be idolized by some in the vampire scene but it is not a prerequisite. One does not need to be a donor to a blood drinker to be accepted into the vampire scene. Should you wish to become a donor or blood drinker, it is essential to follow proper safety precautions. Experienced blood drinkers know how and where to draw blood without permanent damage. Trying to draw blood without an understanding of human anatomy is an invitation for disaster.

At this point it may be worth warning that this book is full of generalizations and intentionally so. In order to explore the various aspects of darkness, which by nature is very internal and personal, one must resort to exploring the commonalities in hopes of grasping the underlying unconscious associations and connections made with their imagery. Nothing in the dark is as clearly defined as it is in light, and this is true with darkness in general. Darksiders come in all shapes, colors, and backgrounds. They may not identify with any of the above mentioned subcultures. Granted they will share certain commonalities, but in no way should they be expected to adhere to a strictly defined standard. The connection runs deeper than physical appearance, and although many will hint of their connection to darkness in their appearance, it should not be assumed all do.

Darkness is mysterious; it is elusive. To define it is to lose its true meaning. Identifying with darkness is not in understanding it, but in acknowledging it within us. In doing so it brings us closer to it, teasing us with its seductive songs of wisdom.

Understanding Darkness

What is "darkness?" Obviously, as Pagans, we are not referring to "evil." Those who would be referred to as darksiders are attuned to the "darker" forces of nature. They tend to be drawn to themes of death, mystery, wisdom, magic, and the night. The moon in all phases is a common symbol.

These themes and symbols are empowering to the darksider because they tap into the deepest reaches of our unconscious. In fact, power itself is often a theme, although it is usually not as readily admitted for fear of misunderstanding[1].

As discussed in the last chapter, although some Pagans are attracted to themes of a darker nature and are collectively referred to as Dark Pagans, there are also many non-Pagan people who are also attracted to these themes. The gothic subculture, for example, is centered around music and aesthetics of dark themes and imagery.

---

[1] For further discussion on this, see chapter on *Power and Darkness*.

Individuals in this scene, called Goths, focus on self-expression and personal freedom. It is this underlying theme of darkness that this chapter will explore. This theme transcends Paganism, encompassing a wide range of attributes, some of which can be considered negative.

Aspects of Darkness

Defining the aspects of "darkness" can be just as difficult and elusive as defining aspects of the goddess/feminine energy as opposed to the god/masculine energy. I have found it easier to determine aspects of darkness by breaking them down into two categories: passive and active. Since polarity is a major theme in many Pagan traditions, I feel this is a good way to approach a definition of darkness.

Basically, the passive aspects of darkness are more in touch with the spiritual/intangible, whereas the active aspects are more in touch with the physical/tangible.

The passive aspects include the moon, wisdom, the night, many generic aspects of the Dark Goddess, mystery, psychic and divinatory work, death, dreams, cemeteries, crossroads, spirits, and magic.

The active aspects include lust, desire, passion, many generic aspects of the Dark God, change, chaos, war/conflict, destruction, storms, sex, wild animals, and the untamable.

Although many aspects can be viewed as being negative (especially in the active aspects), it is the context that determines this. For example, lust, although shunned by many people, is a human urge. It is not sinful or improper in itself. How one handles this urge is the determining factor. Rape would be an example of the misuse of lust. So too with conflict: often it is through conflict that we are able to better ourselves in some way. In a world without conflict our society would stagnate and eventually crumble.

At first glance, one may wish to consider Dark Paganism itself to be passive, and this is definitely a workable generalization when taken as a whole. Dark Paganism IS dark/passive/internal... but just like the Yin-Yang, there is a bit of the other within each.

Those who are attracted to darkness tend to be more introverted. As introverts, they are very self-aware people, more focussed on the internal. They are observers, planners, and thinkers. They are in effect, "self-centered", which in itself is not necessarily a bad trait. A self-centered individual is less likely to get caught up in external concerns such as the perceptions of others. It is only in its extreme form that self-centeredness becomes pretentious and undesirable.

Extroverts, on the other hand, have a tendency to be concerned with external things, focusing attention outward. Those that take the New Age and White Light Paganism to extremes tend to be excessively extroverted, attempting to find all answers via external means such as deities, spirits, crystals, and herbs. Such people are more likely to be driven by underlying feelings of alienation from themselves and others. Their quest for self-awareness can become an unending and unfulfilling cycle as their focus remains on external devices, thus pulling their awareness away from within. By no means does this imply that an extroverted person is unable to have a healthy spiritual life; it simply means that an extroverted individual as a predisposition towards the external and thus often must make more of an effort to focus one's attention inward.

Among the characteristics of those who consider themselves "dark" is often the ability to face one's fears. They strive to look beyond social taboos in an attempt to free themselves from the restrictions of shame and social conditioning. It is because of this that sex is often associated with darkness. The recurrent themes of both death and sex are very personal and highly transformative.

Darkness means different things to different people, but darksiders typically share common associations. Darkness is passionate, seductive, mysterious, powerful. Yet to darksiders, it is also comforting, peaceful, and safe.

Why is darkness seductive? The answer is primarily in that it feeds our innate desire for power and identity. We all want to be someone; we all want a sense of power and control in our lives to some extent. Some acknowledge it while others hide it in shame or deny it outright, but we all feel it at one time or another. Nobody likes to lose – that competitive edge is there inside all of us. Perhaps it is a remnant of our instinct for survival. All the same, it is an aspect of being human.

Darkness makes a connection with this desire. It acknowledges it, accepts it. It does not judge us.

Darksiders also find darkness a source of comfort. To them it is a haven – a place free of the everyday pressures of society, a place where one can drop the masks and defense mechanisms that protect the delicate Self and simply be.

Darkness offers us the opportunity to empower ourselves: to reach for our full potential. It encourages us to free ourselves from the debilitating feelings of shame, fear, guilt, and doubt that bind us through the expectations of our peers, family, society, and culture. It challenges us to be our unadulterated selves – to seek out and obtain that which we desire. Independence, wealth, sexual satisfaction, popularity, acceptance... the list of hidden desires within us is limitless. They may not always be the road to happiness, but acknowledging these often-neglected aspects of ourselves is the road to true personal freedom. We cannot always obtain our desires, and sometimes these desires may become our weaknesses, but we have the right to discover this for ourselves[1] and grow as individuals. It is for this reason that darkness is associated with power. The power does not come from darkness itself but from the realization of the power that we hold within.

Similarly, the mystery associated with darkness is metaphorically associated with the hidden potential within us. When we are faced with the mysterious, the sense of awe awakens our connection to it; we become a part of that mystery.

---

[1] Within reason of course, see chapter on ethics.

Imagery and Archetypes

The recurring imagery of darkness throughout history is deeply rooted within our unconscious minds. These images, such as crossroads and cemeteries, instill a feeling of fear and awe and yet, to those who are attracted to darkness, these images are strangely fascinating and comforting. Such numinous[1] experiences can tell us something essential about ourselves if studied with care.

We all have an inborn predisposition to certain perceptions, feelings, and behaviors that are not dependent upon our individual experiences. Instead, they are inherited as a type of genetic or hard-wired memory. Carl Jung, a Swiss psychoanalyst, called this the *collective unconscious*.

Contained within the collective unconscious are forms called *archetypes*, which represent the possibility of certain types of perceptions and actions. These empty forms develop into actual images through our life experiences.

Archetypes can represent concepts (birth, death, rebirth, magic), beings/entities (mother, child, hero, demon, wise man) or objects (tree, sun, moon, fire, weapon). They unconsciously serve as a frame of reference with which we view the world as well as provide a foundation on which the structure of our personality is built. Archetypes give rise to images in myths and fairy tales both ancient and modern. These myths and stories can be seen as the "acting out" of archetypal images

[1] *Numinous* is a descriptive of persons, situations, or things that have a deep emotional resonance.

where the gods, heroes, and villains represent images of archetypal behavior.

Those who are attuned to darker aspects may find a connection to the characters of myths and stories – be it hero or villain – that are associated with darker imagery. It is through these images and characters that we are able to gain a better insight into the working of our unconscious minds. The following are a few archetypal images and characters associated with darkness. Those who are attracted to dark paths will often identify with many of them.

People drawn to darkness have little modern symbolism in American culture to draw upon other than what Hollywood offers. This symbolism is, of course, biased, being the product of a culture that is afraid of the dark. Thus our youth are easily swayed from viable dark paths into pseudo-satanic trappings and unrealistic occult philosophies and concepts of magic.

Cemeteries

Cemeteries are probably the only constant reminders of our mortality, yet they are peaceful and park-like. Tombstones are often all that remains to mark our existence in a last attempt at immortality. As much as we naturally fear death, those attracted to dark imagery find cemeteries a welcoming retreat from the noise of the outside world. Many cultures outside of North America, such as Mexico and China, frequently visit cemeteries to remember the dead and to tend to the family plots. Mexican cemeteries are much more personalized and non-symmetrical than their North American counterparts.

Death in general is a fascination to many of the people who are attuned to the darker aspects of nature. Yet this morbid fascination tends to instill a certain feeling of comfort. Perhaps in such places we feel less restricted from the constant distractions of this modern age. It offers us a glimpse at the eternal silence that hides within all of us and links us together in the dark. In this silence we find no need for the defense mechanisms we have all created to shield ourselves from one another. When faced with such concrete reminders of our mortality, it is not easy to hide behind our masks of flesh without the realization that there is more to us than the physical. Perhaps this is simply a denial of the possibility of a complete end to our existence, but it also offers us a chance to explore the true nature of our beings. Cemeteries represent death but also the unconscious mind; they symbolize those qualities within us that lie dormant – our hidden potential.

Death

The theme of death is infused into many of the other images of darkness for it is the most powerful of the symbols of darkness. Death is the great inevitable mystery. It is the true cauldron of transformation. In fact, the Death card of the tarot symbolizes change and transformation rather than physical death. For anything to change, something must die or be destroyed. Death itself is what fuels life: we must consume other forms of life to maintain our own. Our own quest for understanding of life and its meaning is encouraged by the fact that we too will one day die. In order for one to spiritually grow or evolve, old concepts of one's self must die.

When faced with death, we naturally try to make sense of it, for that is the nature of being human. But in the end, nothing really ever makes sense of death. We can see it as a natural cycle, but that does not take the tears away when we grieve the death of a loved one. The images associated with darkness and the many forms of the dark deities, especially the Crone, can at least help us to accept death by facing it.

Many run away from it, but where does that leave them in the end? Death is inevitable, and if it holds any answers to what lies beyond it, we'll never truly know for sure until our time comes. Ironically, facing death and accepting it teaches us how to *live*. Perhaps this is why so many darksiders have found the ankh, a looped cross Egyptian hieroglyph meaning "life", such an attractive symbol. The ankh has come to mean "eternal life".

Figure 1: Ankh Hieroglyph

Some cultures, of course, are more accepting of death than others. Octavio Paz, a renowned writer and 1990 Nobel Prize for literature winner, stated "To the resident of New York, Paris, or London, the word DEATH is never pronounced because it burns the lips. Mexicans, on the other hand, frequent it, caress it, they sleep with it, they celebrate it, it is one of their favorite games and their most permanent love."

Crossroads

Crossroads have carried an ominous connotation throughout history and have widely been associated with magic and the appearances of supernatural entities, often attempting to lead lone travelers astray. In classical Europe, offerings of food called "Hecate's supper" were placed at crossroads to propitiate Hecate as well as placate ghosts that could not stay quiet in their graves. In Russia, vampires were believed to lurk at crossroads, attacking travelers at night. In Japan, phallic symbols were placed at road junctions to protect those that passed from the dangers that plagued travelers, while in India offerings were made at crossroads to Rudra, a god who rules ghosts and evil spirits. Crossroads impose upon the traveler a choice of routes, symbolically representing the various paths one's life may take. The outcome of each is unknown, and the wrong choice could prove dangerous. Crossroads also tap into the childhood fear of being lost. Thus crossroads represent the mystery and the unknown we all must face in life.

Ravens/Crows

Ravens and crows are seen in a majority of cultures as harbingers of bad tidings and trickery. Even the words used to describe a group of them (*a murder of crows, an unkindness of ravens*) instill a sense of dread. They are scavengers that feed off the dead and weak and their calls can send chills down one's spine. Haunting the battlefields and feeding on the slain, they have been associated with death since ancient times. Being shy yet extremely crafty creatures, they manifest an air of mystery. Many deities, especially Celtic deities, have been known to take the form of a crow or raven. In Norse mythology, two ravens, Hugin and Munin, served as informants for Odin. The Navajo believed the crow was the messenger of death and the transporter of souls. This ancient mythology was used by James O'Barr to create his graphic novel series (and later influencing a movie and television series), *The Crow*, depicting a vengeful, grief-driven hero returned from the dead to seek justice assisted by a crow that links him to the world of the living.

Although considered birds of ill omen to many, those attuned to darkness tend to find a certain connection with these birds. They can relate in many ways, especially in that they too are often misunderstood and feared by those who cling to the light for protection of the unknown. Of course despite their negative associations, scavengers, such as crows, play an important role in the life cycle that is often ignored.

Skulls/Bones

Like blood, bones are considered by many to be centers of psychic powers. Many cultures believed that life and consciousness remained in them after the death of the original owner and thus it was considered very dangerous to disturb them when they lay in the tomb. The prominence of the skull in bone magic is due to the common belief that the skull is the seat of the soul, just as it was the seat of the mind.

Bones were used in magic and the "witchcraft" of folklore as healing charms and for divination. Mixing powdered bones with red wine, for example, was believed to cure dysentery. Many tribal cultures still use bone fragments for divination similar to how one casts runes.

Today in Madagascar, an ancient ceremony called "*bone-turning*" or "*famadihana*" is still held between June and August, the winter of the Southern Hemisphere, to emphasize the links between the living and the dead. In this ritual, relatives' remains are exhumed, rewrapped in new silk shrouds, and reburied following festive ceremonies in their honor. It is a joyous celebration, which ensures blessings from those whose spirits hover nearby.

A similar festival for the dead found only in Mexico is *Dia de los Muertos* or Day of the Dead, celebrated on November first and second at the same time as All Saints' Day and All Soul's Day. Like the famadihana, the Day of the Dead is a time to remember family members who have died. Cemetery plots are cleaned and decorated, and colorful altars are constructed in homes to honor the dead. Sugar skulls and skeletons are placed on these altars, often with the names of the honored deceased written on them with frosting. After the festivities, these treats are eaten by the children. During the season of the Day of the Dead, decorative paper skeleton figures called *calaveras* of all sizes and made of wood, paper mache, clay, or wax adorn the shops and homes of the Mexican towns. This holiday is not solemn or morbid, but colorful and festive. Mexicans view skeletons as funny and friendly rather than spooky and scary.

Often all that remains of us after death, bones represent our own inevitable death and also the mysteries of what may await us after we shed our corporal forms.

Vampires

The imagery of the vampire reaches deep into the depths of our unconscious. Although fearsome and savage by nature, they captivate us in the form of a deadly romance. Of all the myths, vampires have intrigued us the most. In fact, there have been more adaptations on the vampire myth than any other myth in history. This is perhaps because the vampire, being a very carnal creature, epitomizes our hidden desires. Through the character of the vampire, we can secretly appease that dark side of us that longs for such freedom from restraint. Jung had a theory that we are attracted to certain empowering aspects of our personality that we deny, called our shadow[1]. The vampire represents our shadow – those aspects of us that we cannot face, including our own mortality. The character of the vampire allows us to experience our darker side – the lust, dominance, selfishness – without the guilt associated with it. Therefore, the vampire today is often portrayed as seductive and extremely attractive. Just as our shadow flees from the light of our conscious mind, so too does the vampire flee from the sun.

---

[1] See chapter entitled *"The Shadow"* for a closer examination of this dark side of us.

Wizard/Mage

The wizard or mage holds secret knowledge and great power. He – or she – is mysterious and serious, but often with a childlike sense of humor. This character is almost always old since age and wisdom are strongly tied. Commonly, the appearance of this character is unkempt, alluding to the character's focus on spiritual and intellectual matters over the physical. This powerful individual can be good (teacher or healer) or evil (seeking absolute power and control). The mage satisfies our need for a sense of power or control over a chaotic world. This character's sometimes childlike qualities represent the creative and imaginative child within us that has been forced to "grow up."

Mad Scientist

The mad scientist embodies pure intellect and creativity without moral constraint. Sometimes this character is evil, but more often than not his intentions are good, although his actions end in disaster. Misunderstood and misguided, the mad scientist is often portrayed as charming and sophisticated or with a zany or quirky personality that is almost lovable. The mad scientist is a non-conformist and not afraid to be different, although his unbridled ambition ultimately leads to his downfall. It is through the character of the mad scientist that we can experience the freedom of our creativity that is often set aside for the sake of conformity or lack of the financial stability necessary to focus one's energy completely on one's true goals. How often do our social or employment obligations keep us from following our dreams?

The Monster

This misunderstood creature is usually the unfortunate victim of uncontrollable circumstances such as accident or creation. The Monster attempts to find its place in the world, seeking self-understanding and a sense of identity, but must fight for survival in a world that refuses to accept it. The monster is usually not the initial aggressor, often just wanting to be left alone, but is constantly thrown into situations where it cannot cope. Frankenstein's monster, King Kong, the Phantom of the Opera, the Incredible Hulk, and Edward Scissorhands are all objects of both fear and pity. We relate to the monster in our need to be understood, accepted, or liked by others as well as by ourselves. We share feelings of isolation because of our differences and perhaps, like the monster, harbor a hidden sensitivity.

Seeker of Retribution/Justice

This character has been wronged terribly, and now, blinded or desensitized by his/her pain and suffering, seeks justice in the form of violence. Such a dealer of justice acts with single-mindedness and determination while seeking understanding to the reasons for his or her suffering. This struggle results in the discovery of an internal strength and ultimately the acceptance of one's pain. Characters such as The Crow, Dirty Harry, and Batman allow us to experience our aggressive or violent nature that we often repress. We can relate through our own experiences of being a victim or being wronged. We admire the strength of will these characters use in going against "the system."

Wolf/Werewolf

Due to its cunning and misunderstood nature the wolf has come to be associated with evil. Often the villain in both old fairytales and modern cartoons is often portrayed as a wolf. This association has existed so long in fact that it has made its way into our language in such colloquialisms as "a wolf in sheep's clothing." This association with evil stems from the fact that the wolf's intelligence is quick to remind us that nature is not as inferior and controllable as we would like it to be. Such a creature that dares to remind us of our true place in nature would no doubt be forced to carry such a harsh stigmatism.

The wolf refuses to accept its place in the world as humans see fit to define it. Perhaps this is why the "lone wolves" of our society – the social outcasts, the introverted, the misunderstood – have long identified with the wolf. The wolf is true to its own nature and thus represents the wilderness and the untamable aspects of nature as well as sexuality, an aspect of ourselves we often try to tame.

As an efficient predator, the wolf also represents death. Likewise, as a nocturnal creature known for its tendency to appear to howl at the moon, the wolf is associated with the moon and the night, and thus takes on the attributes of the unconscious, intuition, mystery, magic, and psychic abilities. The strong social skills of the wolf temper some of its harsher attributes with that of nurturing and loyalty. Still, the wolf retains its associations with ferocity and so reminds us that although we need not fear darkness itself, we should not assume there are no hidden dangers.

In light of how the wolf has served as a scapegoat for our own ferocious and destructive nature, it is no surprise that the myth of the werewolf should develop. A man becoming a wolf indirectly links us back to those collective aspects of humanity that we choose to see only in "wild animals." What other animal than man has senselessly destroyed so much? We fear the werewolf because it reminds us of the monster within all of us; the werewolf represents man who has returned to his own animalistic nature.

The Night

The Night represents our unconscious and the mysteries that lurk in our own minds. It is the time we drop our defenses and become vulnerable in sleep. This is the time of dreams and increased psychic awareness – when the unconscious can have its say more freely.

Our Heritage

Before the advent of the electric light, night had much more influence on one's life than it does today. Back then people were forced to flow with the cycle of the sun and moon. The day was the time to work the land and to hunt. As night fell it was a time for the family or tribe to gather around the fire or hearth. It was a time of storytelling and learning. It was the birthing place of the great myths.

The cycle of the seasons played a greater role as well in the lives of our ancestors. During the lighter half of the year the food was grown and hunting was bountiful. The longer days allowed time for the work to be done. As the darker half of the year approached, harvest began and food was preserved and stored for the coming winter.

Winter brought darkness and cold. The land no longer could be worked and so life centered on the home. It was a time for families and neighbors to gather.

At the same time, night instilled fear. It was not considered safe to travel at night and all cultures had their tales of strange creatures that lurked in the darkness.

Without electric lights, the nights of the past were truly dark and foreboding. Torches could only light a small area leaving the bearer surrounded by a sea of black. Traveling was limited to nights when the moon was full and the sky was clear. Both animal and human predators made use of the darkness to prey on hapless travelers.

The Present

There is an isolated area on the far west side of New York City just below West 14th Street known as the "meat packing district." As the name implies, this area consists mostly of warehouses and meat wholesale outlets. One would imagine that at night this area would be deserted, but after midnight its darker aspects begin to show. Tucked away behind graffiti-strewn gates and reinforced steel doors lie several leather/S&M sex clubs; a club catering to the gothic, vampiric, and fetish scenes; numerous seedy gay clubs, many with infamous back rooms; a biker club; and other clubs of various alternative tastes. Amidst the stench of urine and butcher shops, scantily clad transvestite and transgender prostitutes of the most unappealing sort haunt many of the corners[1].

It is truly a secret world of decadence and perversion where many unspeakable activities occur. Yet, as the sun rises and the shadows retreat to the alleyways and the gates and doors close, the very nature of this area changes. As people scurry to work they pass these hidden venues without the slightest awareness of what they pass.

Today, the night still holds its intrigue, although its hold on us is often much more subtle. The night is when the doors to the underground are opened. Various subcultures – gothic, vampiric, fetish, and combined variations – find havens in which to celebrate their connection to darkness.

The night is also a lonely time. Many seek these underground havens hoping to find meaning or a sense of connection and community. Others seek sex in the back of porn shops and alleys, hoping for even the momentary release from loneliness that orgasm or a high provides. Walk through the streets of any large community in the pre-dawn hours and you will find the lost and abandoned of society.

Darksiders find solace in the silence and cover of the night. There is a certain thrill to walking

---

[1] Sadly this particular area has slowly lost its dark charm over the last few years, being taken over by the more mundane. Still, such places exist, if only in smaller pockets tucked inconspicuously around the city.

through the desolate streets of a city or town late at night when the windows are dark and the streets are empty. These places have a completely different personality at night. Without the buzz of daytime activity, one can hear the subtle sounds of the night: the hum of the street lamps, the clanking of the pulleys on a flagpole in the wind, the rustling of the wind in the trees and over rooftops. Such things are found to be empowering. As the world seems to sleep, our creativity awakens. It is unfortunate that many of us have been forced to adjust to a life centered on the day so that as night falls, our bodies expect sleep and our minds begin to cloud.

To some these images instill a sense of loneliness and longing, and indeed the night harbors such things, but to the children of the night there is also comfort. At night, we find ourselves closer to the silence within all of us that links us together.

Evil

Evil is a very complicated area to discuss. The concepts vary among individuals and religions, although evil has absolutely nothing to do with Dark Paganism, or with Paganism in general for that matter. In fact, evil is not, as many people like to believe, an aspect of darkness: it can exist on both sides of the light/dark polarity.

There are several reasons why evil has been categorized as dark. On the one hand, evil, being feared, is categorized along with many of the more destructive or misunderstood aspects of darkness that are also feared by many white-light paths. On the other hand, the various dark paths are more likely to address the issue of evil instead of labeling it and then avoiding or ignoring the issue. "Darksiders," as those who walk dark paths and lifestyles are commonly called, are willing to explore that which has been labeled "evil" by others in order to make an educated decision on how to view or handle it. However, since evil is often associated with the category of "darkness," albeit on a more negative side, a discourse on darkness would be incomplete without examining the concept of evil.

There is no universally accepted definition of evil. Some feel it is a complete lack of ethics, while others believe it is an actual force. One's religious belief or culture will often determine the definition. Christians, for example, personify evil as "Satan" and thus view evil as a force that tempts mankind into acts of self-destruction. This concept of an external manifestation of evil is necessary for aggressively dualistic religions that believe that the deity is a manifestation of absolute good. Therefore, such religions tend to have moral codes interwoven into the religious beliefs. Pagan traditions, having a more pantheistic approach to the deities, tend to avoid such opposing dualism and thus prefer to keep moral codes and religious beliefs somewhat more separate and personal.

Pagans tend to avoid the word "evil" due to the term's strong ties to Christianity. The word "evil" tends to insinuate an external force, and since this does not tend to fit well in most Pagan belief systems, words such as "unethical" or "abusive" are found to be more suitable. Instead of an external force, evil is seen by most Pagans as an internal imbalance or sickness.

Unfortunately, many of the more extreme White-light Pagans still cling to the term "evil", especially when attempting to define dark paths because they have not yet broken free of the Judeo-Christian-Islamic conditioning of their childhood. These tend to be the very types of Pagans that Dark Pagans disdain for their often unrealistic or hypocritical stance on Paganism. Of course, not all White-light Pagans are extremists that deny the existence and necessity of darkness, but there has been a disturbing trend lately toward the more shallow influences of the New Age movement.

Taken simply in the context of "darkness," evil encompasses the more unjustifiably destructive aspects of darkness as well as the excessive use of these darker aspects. As mentioned earlier in the example of lust, it can become "evil" when it is abused. Lust itself is not evil; but when it leads to stalking or rape, evil would be a good description of that abuse. However, evil in this sense is not limited to darkness, although it is often associated with darkness due to its more carnal nature. It would be more accurate to say that Darksiders are more *aware* of their sometimes-evil nature while Lightsiders are more likely to avoid that acceptance or insist that it can be conquered. Therefore, the evil found in Lightsiders tends to be masked by excuses such as "good intentions" or "outside influences" since they refuse to own it. As will be examined in the next chapter, this can have drastic consequences.

The Shadow

Locked away within each of us is a terrible beast worthy of our most potent fear and loathing. Anyone who has seriously searched for better self-understanding has no doubt come to realize that there are some urges and feelings we prefer not to claim as our own. These same traits, it turns out, are often the very ones we tolerate least in others.

Perhaps we try to remove these feelings, as if they are a sickness that can be healed by prayer and meditation. Or perhaps we just choose to look the other way, hoping they will return to the darkness that seemed to spawn them. Some claim that "radiant light" will destroy this darkness, as it does in fairy tales. But this is the real world, and those ideas are nothing more than a security blanket.

Welcome, sojourner, for your journey has just begun. The Fool of the tarot is about to wizen up, or else remain the fool, secure in his or her ignorance.

A Brief Background

Before exploring the concept of the shadow, it would help to have a basic understanding of the principles of psychology that eventually helped us to grasp this powerful archetypal force. (Don't worry, this will be short and painless!)

Sigmund Freud (1856-1939), the creator of psychoanalysis, was the first person to scientifically explore the human unconscious mind. His model of the mind consisted of three parts: the ego, id, and superego. The ego is what we think as being our true self. It is comprised of all the ordinary thoughts and functions needed to direct a person in one's daily behavior. The id is mostly unconscious and contains all our instincts as well as everything that was repressed into it by the superego – our conscience or ideal self, so to speak. The superego harbors the values, ideals, and prohibitions that set the guidelines for the ego. It is the judge or censor of the ego, punishing through the imposition of feelings of guilt and anxiety. In essence, the superego is our moral conscience.

Later, a student of Freud named Carl Gustav Jung (1875-1961) developed his own theories based on his adaptations of Freud's model of the mind and came to develop what is known as analytical psychology. Jung felt that Freud's emphasis in psychoanalysis on erotic factors led to a one-sided, reductionistic view of human motivation and behavior. Instead, Jung looked towards myths and dreams in relation to the human psyche and recognized the link between symbols and psychology.

What Freud referred to as "the repressed" gave birth to what Jung saw as the shadow. From the standpoint of psychology, the shadow is basically the disowned or repressed self, the alter ego, or the id.

What is the Shadow?

Simply put, the shadow is that part of us that we have disowned through repression to the point that we are no longer consciously aware of its existence. It is that part of our personality that has been sacrificed for the sake of the ideal ego. Although this includes our cheating, dishonest, and violent sides, it may also contain traits that are constructive.

The roots of the shadow run deep and can never fully be explored in one's lifetime. It begins as soon as we learn to relate to the world around us. Every time we are told that something is wrong, sinful, shameful, or is deemed in any way unacceptable, we push it off into the shadow. As children, these pressures first came from our parents and then teachers. As we began to mature, the pressure of our peers and society also took their toll as we attempted to fit in and adapt. We all know how cruel the playground can be as a child and how harsh the ridicule of our peers can be should we fail to be accepted by them.

In the workplace, we soon learn that we often must compromise our personal goals to succeed. Dreams and ambitions that are considered foolish or impractical are set aside, as is our spirituality. The workplace influences us to behave in certain ways in order to adapt and succeed, often undermining personal values in the process.

Unfortunately, not everything that was discarded was negative. Creativity, sensitivity, and spontaneity are often lost to the shadow in the process. Sometimes what is considered a limitation or fault simply does not measure up to society's stereotypical expectations of what is "normal." The more we conform to the dictates of our surroundings, the more we are forced to repress.

It is important to understand that this repression is usually an autonomic response. Although we may at times make a conscious effort to block certain negative thoughts and emotions, the shadow has in essence a life of its own running in tandem with the ego; each creates itself from the same life experiences. The fact is that we are not usually aware of our shadow aspects since the ego unconsciously denies their existence.

The traits relegated to the shadow are an innate part of us – if we are born with a predisposition towards violence we will always have a violent aspect in us. We may learn to control such impulses, but they still exist; like it or not, they are a part of us. Accepting the existence of such aspects allows us to better handle these feelings as they arise.

The Power of the Shadow

As mentioned above, although the shadow may contain constructive elements of our personality, it primarily consists of our inferiorities – those aspects of our nature that we have consciously or unconsciously rejected due to moral, religious, cultural, or even aesthetic considerations. Since we are unable to accept these aspects as our own, they are so well repressed that we see them indirectly in how we perceive others. In essence, we project these traits onto others that show even the slightest sign of those attributes. Homophobes, for example, often hide within their anger and fear their own unrealized sensitivity that they have mistaken as being too feminine ("real men don't cry", etc.) or themselves harbor confused homosexual feelings that they refuse to accept. By attacking homosexuality in others, they attempt to symbolically destroy the homosexual tendencies or stereotypical homosexual traits that lie within themselves.

We instinctually lash out against this threat often in what would seem to others to be an overreaction. Similarly, those negative qualities we find forgivable and do not excessively disturb us are less likely to be part of our shadow.

When we see something or someone as "the enemy," we are often projecting our shadow onto it. The classmate or co-worker you just can't stand – whose every action is an annoyance – is a good indicator that something internal is not clicking right.

These projections may appear as a threat to one's established values. In fact, the more one perceives oneself as perfect or in the right, the more likely one will be to project one's shadow onto others. This is exactly why fundamentalist Christians are so adversely against Pagans. It is also why many staunchly white-light Pagans are so negative towards darker paths: they *need* an adversary to fight against in order to justify or empower their cause. Ignorance only feeds the projections. Many New-Age adherents have gone to such extremes as to ignore the contributions of destruction, resulting in a very plastic semblance of spirituality. They become isolated, relating to the world through the illusions their projections create. Spirituality based solely on light and love has no depth.

Because we fear that acknowledging these dark urges will either force us to act them out or leave us frustrated by not satisfying them, we find repression to be easier than discipline. However, repression is more dangerous because it forces us to act without consciousness of our motives. Repression is nothing more than looking away. The shadow *will* be heard – if not in one's consciousness, then in one's unconscious actions. Left to its own devices in the unconscious, the shadow fuels self-destructive patterns in our behavior – it sabotages our judgment with clouded concepts of "good intentions." As the old adage goes, *that which we cannot face will surely catch us from behind.*

Collective Shadow

The shadow and its projections not only affect us individually, but also collectively. Every society – every nation – has an identity of its own to which we relate. This group mentality creates its own shadow whereby people identify with an ideology or leader that gives expression to their fears and inferiorities as a whole, giving rise to religious or racial persecution, witch hunting, scapegoating, and genocide. The collective shadow is the root of social, racial, and national bias and discrimination; every minority and dissenting group carries the shadow projections of the majority.

Great destruction has been done in the name of patriotism and righteousness under the illusion of the projections of the collective shadow. Nazi Germany and Apartheid in recent times, and the Crusades and "witch hunts" of our past, are good examples of the power of the collective shadow over an entire nation.

It is perhaps the greatest irony of all that the most senseless destruction – if not evil – occurs when a society or individual attempts to destroy "evil." The focus on this evil is always misplaced. Instead of destroying the sickness within themselves, they seek to destroy anything that reminds them of their own failings through projection. This is an unconscious defense mechanism, fueled by the refusal to accept the possibility that the blame lies within, not without. When there are no others on which to project, Satan and demons were (and still are) useful scapegoats.

Historically, demons have served as default scapegoats for a variety of unacceptable or inadequate emotions or impulses. They focus blame away from the Self to an outside, uncontrollable source, opening the way for all sorts of projection. The use of demons as a scapegoat was so great before the 17th century that it was believed that emotional disorders and insanity were literally caused by them.

It is interesting to point out that during what has come to be known as the "burning times[1]", the church taught that even negative thoughts were sins. Since it is impossible to completely control our negative thoughts and emotions, repression ran deep in the common folk. It is no surprise that much energy was put into searching for and destroying witches, who served as scapegoats for their own feelings of rage, jealousy, greed, lust, and murderous intentions that lay just beneath the surface, masked by their "proper selves." Thus, many attacked evil as a self-defense against insight into the self. Such defense mechanisms are still quite common today.

Projection does not in any way excuse us from our actions. Although we cannot be held responsible for our thoughts, we *are* responsible for our actions. Hitler, Pol Pot, Stalin, and other such "hideous" leaders have risen to power by feeding the collective projections of their societies. They were relatively "normal" people brought into (and kept in) power by the support of others. Hitler, for example, may go down in history as the root of all evil of Nazi Germany, but what of the men, women, and children who enthusiastically cheered on their leader? Those who distributed pro-Nazi flyers and discussed politics of a better Germany over coffee? Perhaps they did not know the whole truth, but enough was self-evident to know that there were injustices being performed. Yet, somehow it seemed justifiable at the time. Perhaps the only redeeming value of their actions is in the reminder that it can happen again as the "ethnic cleansing" of Kosovo of recent times demonstrates.

---

[1] Today this term refers to witch persecutions regardless of the means.

Today in our "civilized society" war hides behind the guise of peace keeping, of military strikes and sanctions, and in military presence. Are these the tools of peace or the acts of war? In the end, it all depends on one's perspective. But who is right? History shows it to be the majority, the victor, the strongest – for they are the ones who write the history books. In the real world, sometimes the only distinction between the "good guys" and the "bad guys" is in who is telling the story. After all, what is propaganda but food for the collective shadow?

Today we watch the news and see other nations as the enemy. We are so quick, in the distant comfort of our homes, to pass judgment with just a few minutes of biased facts. How much of viewpoint is projection fed by propaganda? Sometimes things are not as cut and dried as we like to think.

I see Saddam Hussein as an insane leader of a nation of radical zealots. They see the United States as a bully nation. Although I don't discount the dangers Saddam poses to us, how much do I really know about him? Yet still I sneered at someone handing out pro-Iraqi literature during rush hour in New York City, not even bothering to hear his view. Where does projection end and the truth begin? How many of us can honestly say they unbiasedly researched the situation before passing judgment? The truth is, very few, and in acknowledging that we have taken the first step in confronting the collective shadow.

Confronting the Shadow

A confrontation with the shadow is essential in the development of self-awareness. Such encounters are often referred to with metaphors such as "meeting our demons," "the dark night of the soul", or "midlife crisis." At some point in our lives we will no doubt experience a time when we suddenly discover that we do not like who we have become. We may feel guilt or shame as we reflect over some of our past actions and motives. We may discover that we have lived the life of a hypocrite. Chances are that it will be a very negative and biased encounter where we become too depressed to see the positive aspects of our lives.

To many this happens at mid-life when we come to the inevitable conclusion that life is on the wane. We begin to rethink our past and ponder our future. We start to assess our accomplishments to find where we stand in life. In doing so, we also come to see that we have not lived up to our own standards. We are not the same people we present ourselves to the world as being. Of course such a realization can happen at any age, and those who are more reflective in nature (such as most darksiders) will face this dilemma many times in their lives.

The often depressive, dark motifs of those who walk a dark spiritual path or lifestyle are quite symbolic of the confrontation of the shadow. Any confrontation with the shadow means the death of some aspect of our ego, for the ego is our ideal self – how we see ourselves and how we want to be seen by others. When we suddenly find an awareness of the shadow (our alter ego) we discover that within us are the very things we despise the most. Our egocentric defenses begin to fall apart, resulting in temporary depression or a clouding of consciousness. We are not what we like to think we are, and being presented with this reality can be earth-shattering. There is suddenly this deep fear that the person we know as ourselves will be destroyed and that all we have built in our lives will be lost.

Confrontation with the shadow is not simply a question of admitting to our faults, but a question of being shaken right down to the very core of our being by the realization that we are not what we appear to be – not only to others, but also to ourselves. What we value most will be severely bruised if we accept what the shadow has to show us.

As depressing as such encounters with the shadow are, it is an essential phase in the attainment of true self-awareness and spiritual growth. Confrontation with the shadow is the greatest obstacle on such a journey. Many fall prey to the shadow's projections and hide behind its illusions of victory over evil. Sadly, the object to spiritual growth is not in the victory over "evil," but in the acceptance that we are a part of it. We should not give in to destructive tendencies, but we should also not lose touch with these feelings; to deny *any* aspect of ourselves is to deny ourselves of a true sense of wholeness.

Carl Jung once said, "I would rather be whole than good." This is the key to survival when confronting the shadow, for life consists of achieving good not *apart* from "evil" but *in spite of it*. Despite our sometimes negative urges, we should strive for some semblance of decency. The more aware we are of such urges, the better we are able to consciously choose our direction. We may not be able to control our feelings, but we *can* control our actions when we understand the motivational forces behind them.

But how does one confront something we instinctually deny? There are several ways, although each requires time and patience.

Over-Reaction Journal

Keep a journal of all the times you have over-reacted or were made very upset or angry. Try to recall important details, such as the context of the situation and who was there. Did you feel the need to defend yourself by constantly explaining your intentions? Did you find yourself denying a perceived accusation? Did you take things out of perspective?

Before retiring that evening, reflect over the journal entries for the day. Do you see any patterns in the situations that warranted an entry? Do the events center on anyone in particular?

Examine closely the people and types of situations that seem to elicit a strong response. They have probably triggered an unconscious defense mechanism through projection of the shadow. Since we unconsciously refuse to acknowledge the existence of the shadow, its characteristics are often projected onto others. Once the focus has been taken away from ourselves we perceive the recipient of the projection as a threat or enemy, often reacting to it in an overly hostile way.

If we are quick to deny something, then it is very likely that it has struck a chord in the unconscious mind and somehow brought us closer to our shadow. Be open-minded and try to examine your reactions more closely. What is it about a certain person that irritates or repels you? What is the perceived threat?

A good rule of thumb in identifying a projection is that if a person or thing *informs* us then there is probably no projection in place. However, if it *affects* us, then there is a strong chance that we are the victims of our own projection. In other words what we see in others is more-or-less correct if it simply informs us, but if it strongly affects us emotionally then there is a good chance that there is more going on in our unconscious than simple observation. For example, if someone cuts in front of me in traffic and I simply think to myself "that was rude" then I am probably not projecting. On the other hand, if someone were to cut in front of me and I took it as a personal offence, then I could be projecting the fact that I too, have a tendency of acting without concern for others either on or off the road.

Once you have found the answers, look within and see how these traits relate to you. Have there been instances where you have shown or been accused of possessing these very traits? Do you feel the need to justify those instances? Congratulations! You've just made contact with one of your shadow traits. Accept that it is a part of you and move on. This in no way makes you less of a person. On the contrary, it makes you more of a *whole* person.

Recognizing the Inner Voices

Using the same journal as described above, try to recognize the underlying voices that guided your perception. Meditate on these inner voices and try to vocalize them. Let go and blurt out everything that comes to mind. Let the voices trigger the same emotional response they triggered before but let it flow freely. Don't be frightened at the automatic outpouring that may follow. Let it have its say.

Once the voices have been expressed, answer the voices back. Challenge the dictates and content of the voice. Record what was said in your journal for later reflection (you may want to make use of a tape recorder if this will not make you too self-conscious). Try to track down that inner-critic to understand where those feelings stemmed.

Active Imagination/Expression

The goal of active imagination is to get in touch with the unconscious by giving it an opportunity to express itself. To do this one must learn to clear the mind of its conscious clutter and allow the fantasies and voices that are always present in the unconscious mind to come into consciousness.

There are many ways of letting the unconscious express itself, such as through movement, music, or art. Movement is often the most effective means of expressing the unconscious, particularly through dance, but it is also the hardest to keep a record of for later examination. As with recalling dreams, things that come from the unconscious have a tendency to just as quickly disappear from the conscious mind.

Start by creating a supportive environment, perhaps formally casting a circle. Take all measures possible to ensure you will not be disturbed. Sit or lay comfortably and relax, following your breath. When you have reached a meditative state, visualize yourself being somewhere you find peaceful, be it real or imaginary. Focus on the details, such as the scents and sounds around you. Try to include all of your senses (feel the wind, etc.). Feel the power and sacredness of this place and let it empower you.

When you have made a connection with this safe place, visualize the presence of the one person in your life – past or present – that you would least like to see, someone who greatly annoys or disgusts you. Concentrate on seeing and hearing whatever comes up from the unconscious. Observe the person. What is he or she doing or saying? What is this person wearing?

Note how you feel. What is it about this person that is so offensive? Take a few moments to fully experience this figure from your shadow. Let your feelings flow free.

With your eyes still closed, begin to express your feelings with the medium you have chosen. Begin to draw, write, or dance – whatever you need to do to freely express yourself. When you are ready, slowly open your eyes and continue to work on your expression for about 15 minutes. Don't try to make sense of it yet, but let it out freely. Be spontaneous. Stay with the feeling of the visualization. Don't let yourself become concerned with judging the quality of your work. If you chose to express yourself through dance, try to record the pattern of the movements or find words to describe them.

Although you may not understand the significance of the images or movements, the simple act of expressing is healing since you now have a conscious image of your shadow to work with. At a later time revisit the record of your expression and meditate on its significance. Record what feelings you experience while doing this.

Ask an Observer

One of the best ways of getting insight on oneself, especially on aspects that are elusive to one's own consciousness, is to ask someone else. This person should be someone very close and trustworthy and who has agreed to take this effort seriously. Keep in mind, however, that such a venture can tax a relationship, which is why many prefer to work with a therapist.

Have the person verbally list your bad habits and hypocritical behavior, noting your reactions. Anything that seems to elicit an emotional response or severe denial should be explored further since they no doubt hint at one's own shadow qualities. Ask the friend for elaboration if necessary, but stop when things start to get out of hand, especially since the friend will probably not know how to handle the emotions that may be released. It is very important to maintain a supportive environment.

Later, while alone, review the notes made by the observer and try to see those notes objectively.

Why did you insist on redirecting the blame? Why did some items get you so upset?

The use of a therapist as the observer has advantages in that the therapist is trained in the art of active listening and can help redirect focus back onto you as you project the blame onto others. Of course, to establish such a relationship with a therapist to the point that he or she can know you well enough to see these shadow traits will take time, but can be well worth it.

An Indirect Approach

Writing poetry and stories are also useful tools in letting the unconscious have its say, especially for those who have trouble contacting the unconscious directly. Stories, especial about other people, often reveal parts of the storyteller's own psyche. The characters in such stories are able to act out parts of the shadow without threatening the storyteller's sense of self.

Look for patterns in the themes of your writing. Are there hidden messages? What is it about the imagery or characters that intrigues or disturbs you?

Dreams

Dreams are often direct communications from the unconscious and thus can be very useful in shadow work. Keep a diary of all nightmares and disturbing or powerful dreams. Try to note details such as characters and settings, and most importantly the emotions associated with the dream. To do this, it is best to write about dreams immediately upon awakening since the images will quickly fade. (It comes in handy to keep a pad and pen near your bed for this.)

The shadow often manifests itself as a character of the same sex as the dreamer, although any characters that elicit an emotional response should be noted. As with similar journals, take some time to reflect on the entries and locate patterns.

Individuation: Becoming Whole

As mentioned above, although our first reaction is to avoid or destroy our shadow, this is pointless. Ignoring or fighting the shadow with willpower alone only relegates its power to the unconscious, where it exerts its power – unbeknownst to us – in a negative, compulsive projected form. The shadow *cannot* be eliminated, and it is most powerful and dangerous when we think that we have conquered it.

We cannot change who we are. We can improve ourselves in many ways, but our nature remains constant. Those aspects of ourselves, which we wish to disown never go away, but we can discipline ourselves to act in a manner that is sometimes contrary to our feelings and desires. We need to re-channel the energy of the shadow, and to do so requires both an awareness of the shadow and the acceptance that it cannot simply be gotten rid of.

Shadow-work is the intentional process of admitting to ourselves that which we have thus far chosen to repress or ignore and taking account of our destructive side. This is the first step towards *individuation* – the process of becoming whole by accepting and integrating the shadow as part of us.

When first encountering one's shadow, the person feels depressed and doomed since the ego sees this as a defeat. The truth can be very overwhelming at first, but in time this insight brings us closer to the *Self*: the word Jung used to define our creative center. Eventually, the "true center" of our personality begins to emerge and the ego (our sense of self) is gradually reoriented to a closer relationship with that true center[1].

Such an experience makes us much more realistic about ourselves. We learn to accept the dark impulses within us, understanding that to be human is to be full of longing and contradictions. It would be foolish to think that a committed spiritual life would protect us from human suffering.

One of the most direct paths to individuation is through consciously confronting the shadow. But facing and owning the attributes of the shadow is not an easy task. It is a painful process, for although the shadow can contain positive elements of our personality that we can reclaim as our own, it consists primarily of our inferiorities – the primitive and awkward aspects of our nature that we have long since rejected. The depression

---

[1] This concept of two centers of one's personality distinguishes Jungian psychology from practically all other psychologies: the ego being the center of our consciousness and the Self being the center of our total personality which includes the ego, consciousness, and the unconscious.

that follows may seem crippling, but such a depressive state turns us inward, allowing us a deeper communication with our wholeness – the Self.

Confronting our shadow – our hypocritical self, the inner critic – is a very humbling experience, and also a growing experience. When you can recognize your shadow qualities you can then incorporate the more positive hidden attributes such as power, sexuality, assertiveness, or even gentleness and sensitivity to expand your sense of self. You also find more control over those qualities that are not socially acceptable since you are now aware of them. Awareness helps keep such negative attributes from secretly surfacing in actions misguided by our unconscious.

When we have the courage to confront our shadow aspects, they change. The negative aspects do not need to take over our personality, as we fear that they will do; they simply need to be heard and acknowledged. We need to own up to our disowned aspects. Only then can they lessen their destructive grip on our behavior. It is ironic that we are so reluctant to confront our dark side in fear that it will overpower us, when just the opposite is true. We end up following the dictates of the shadow only when we give it free reign in our unconscious through repression.

By confronting our shadow we also take responsibility for much of our own discord in life. The discomforts that the shadow inflicts on us – guilt, fear, anxiety, depression – are actually discomforts we are inflicting on *ourselves*. Slowly our projections break down and we find that much of the blame for our woes that we have projected on the world actually stemmed from within. We must reverse these projections in order to own them. What we thought the environment was doing to us is often something we are doing to ourselves. For example, if I feel guilt I may claim that I am a victim of the people or circumstances that are inflicting this feeling of guilt onto me, when in reality that guilt came from within – it was *my* reaction caused by *my* perception. Although it may have been unconscious, the feeling of guilt and the associated suffering and mental anguish came from within. As insane and chaotic as the world may be, we are not the victims of it as much as we may think we are. Once we break free of the illusory world of our projections and take responsibility for our feelings, we are able to truly find freedom: that which we have run from proves to be the source of our redemption.

Taking It Too Far

Confronting and accepting the shadow may be important in becoming whole, but over-identifying with the shadow is just as dangerous as avoiding it. Wholeness cannot emerge if any portion of our Self is ignored. Attempting to destroy the ego for the sake of the shadow invites moral and mental instability. In seeking to better understand the shadow, we should not forsake or discount our more conscious aspects, as they are necessary for us to effectively exist in society.

Some dark paths may overemphasize our dark side, but this is only to combat the popular mindset of repression. Much of our shadow is self-defeating, and thus deserves to remain controlled. Not all of it can be harnessed for our benefit. The point of shadow-work is *not* to release these negative aspects but to discover and acknowledge them so that they no longer control us unconsciously. We should neither give in nor lose touch with our destructive tendencies. Knowing our shadow-aspects gives us more control over our actions and a true sense of personal freedom.

The process of individuation recognizes the totality of being, which consists of the *complementing* polarities of light and dark, creation and destruction, rational and irrational, good and evil, masculine and feminine, and conscious and unconscious that exist in a fluctuating state in our psyche. When we choose to block out one side for the other we upset our internal balance. We all have within each of us both aspects of these polarities, and it is only by embracing both sides that are we able to use them appropriately.

On "Demons" and "Evil Spirits"

While writing the first draft of this book I had the opportunity to share my ideas with many people of various Pagan paths and occult backgrounds.

Despite my treatise on evil in a Pagan context, I was still asked about the existence of "demons" and the use of black magic, and also reminded to warn my readers of the dangers of working with some of the more destructive or untamable aspects of darkness.

At first I felt that this was exactly what I was avoiding. After all, Pagans, including "Dark Pagans", are nature-based. Therefore, *technically* most Pagans would not believe in demons, let alone accept the concept of evil as an actual force.

Still, many Pagans *do* believe in or have experienced such energies, and so I need to explore this subject further. After all, Dark Pagans are supposed to be the ones who dare enter the shadows to better understand that which is often feared. Just because we find in such exploration that there is often no need to fear the dark and mysterious does not mean that there are not dangers lurking there as well. It would be foolish of me to deny the risks. Life itself has its risks, be it in the light or in the darkness. Dark Pagans are more likely to take risks and accept the consequences of their actions and learning from their mistakes.

So then, how does a nature based spirituality – either dark or light – acknowledge the existence of demons and evil spirits if the nature of those entities contradicts the foundation of Pagan beliefs?

First of all, let us explore the concept of deity in Paganism. Generally speaking, nature-based spritualties view deities as aspects of the creative – *and destructive* – forces of nature. Many of the darker deities are therefore attuned to these destructive forces. These deities are wild, more intense, sometimes overwhelming, and thus demand a more cautious approach. A wise practitioner would not, for example, invoke Loki the same way one would invoke Aphrodite. The energies are very different and that must be taken into context when working with the deities. Therefore, although these darker deities need not be avoided, they should be approached with caution and, above all, respect. The basic rule of thumb is if you don't feel a certain affinity towards a deity, you probably should not be working with it at that time.

Secondly, certain magical traditions, such as Chaos Magic, believe that the deities are created by the practitioner. Using deities that already exist allows one to draw upon the collective energies of those who have focused their own energies on such deities through worship and magic workings as well as the archetypal images they represent in our own psyche. In this sense, existing deities are ancient archetypes that have, through centuries of worship and/or invocation, become self-actuated. As an old saying goes, "the gods die when they are forgotten." Although not all would accept that all deities have been created by humans, popular magical theory accepts the possibility of creating entities (such as elementals) by relying on such concepts of human potential.

What we call "demons" therefore, can exist as malicious entities just as guardian spirits can exist as beneficent entities. They, as with deities, are storehouses of a specific form – or frequency – of energy that can be tapped into to increase the potency of magic.

Many religions and traditions, including some forms of Christianity, utilize such theories. One would, in Catholicism for example, pray to Saint Anthony to locate lost objects or Saint Christopher for safe travel for these are the associated patron saints. (Patron saints are chosen as special protectors or guardians over various areas of life such as occupations, illnesses, or causes.)

Therefore, "demons" and "evil spirits" do exist, although from the viewpoint of Pagans, they are simply archetypal energies associated with the more destructive aspects of nature or the human psyche. They are the spiritual manifestations of human hate and fear. Evil *can* exist as a force, but it is a force created and directed by humans with the intention to cause harm. It is not so much an aspect of nature as a whole as it is an aspect of humanity; evil exists because humans will it to exist.

Protecting Ourselves

We are constantly bombarded with psychic energy from the thoughts and emotions of those around us, as well as from locations such as sacred or haunted places that are natural reservoirs for certain types of energies. Even objects resonate with energy (hence the use of talismans made from natural objects). All humans, be it the most adept magical practitioner or the completely clueless, have a natural psychic shielding. Just as one must be open to the deities to receive their gifts, so too must one be open to malicious deities to be harmed. Fear, doubt, hate – these feelings provide the cracks in our natural psychic shielding for these malicious energies or entities to enter. They feed on the superstition and fear that is often lurking in our unconscious until faced with the possibility of such a threat. The effectiveness of a protection spell or ritual is often due more to the feeling of security one obtains by performing it than from the energies that are actually raised.

Hence, a "curse" is often effective because the "victim" allows it through fear. Often, victims are oblivious to the fact that a curse was placed on them until it was made known to them by the sender. Ironically, just the claim of a curse can be enough to set its effects in motion, even if no actual magic was performed!

Although we all have a natural shielding it is limited, and so direct assaults from malicious entities or focused negative energy by competent practitioners have a greater possibility of influencing the victim's life in some (usually subtle) way. Fortunately, those who feel the need to play with such forces tend to lack the maturity and discipline necessary to perform effective magic. It is for this reason that such effective attacks are not common.

There are several methods of protecting oneself from malicious psychic influences, be they actual attacks or random encounters. One of the most common methods is through visualization. By visualizing a shield of energy around the body (typically in the form of a sphere of light) we consciously strengthen our natural defenses. This form of shielding visualization can be done during a meditation, during the course of a protection ritual, or simply while commuting to work or upon entering a room where hostility is sensed.

Visualization can also be used within the constructs of a ritual[1] to redirect deliberate attacks back to the sender. Although this works best when the assailant is known, such attacks can still successfully be returned through visualization. To do this, take a moment to sense the antagonistic force while working within a circle or other sacred or empowering space. Try to get a feel for the character of this malignant energy. What color is it? What images are associated with it? What form does it take in your mind's eye? Once a strong image of the attacking energy has been established, redirect that energy towards that image with the intention of returning it to its source. Redirection can then be followed by a binding spell, which binds the sender from causing more harm. As with the above process, visualize either the attacker, if known, or the image that attacking force manifests in your

---

[1] See chapter entitled the *Structure of Magic* for more information on how to work with magic.

senses. Visually bind that image with your own will so that the sender can no longer direct negativity back to you. For added symbolism, one can also wrap a candle or other physical representation of the attacker with a cord while using this binding visualization.

The Enemy Within

Of course, sometimes, attacks by malevolent forces do not come from an outside agent or entity. Sometimes, the demons that plague us are our own. As was discussed in the chapter entitled *"The Shadow,"* aspects of ourselves which we fear or abhor are often repressed into our unconscious where, if ignored, they can manifest through the way we see others or situations. When this dark side of us is ignored, we unconsciously project it onto people or circumstances. We then see those people as our enemy (or in some way irritating) and those circumstances as "bad luck" or manifestations of some malevolent force.

Encounters with these would-be demons, are likely to occur during dreams, meditations or astral work where the unconscious mind, not willing to accept our dark side as part of us, instead sees it as a demon or malevolent entity. Such experiences tend to elicit a strong sense of fear or loathing that probably appears as an overreaction to others. Instead of fighting these "personal demons" one must confront them to discover what aspects of ourselves we have grown accustomed to repressing. Banishing such demons will prove ineffective in the long run since the more we repress our shadow (dark side), the stronger an influence it will have in our unconscious and thus the less control we will have of it.

Obviously the way we handle our personal demons is completely different from how we would handle an actual encounter with a malicious entity of some sort and not easy to differentiate. Thus the reason the novice to magic is warned of its dangers. Any serious practitioner has no doubt heard the saying *"know thyself."* The path of spirituality and/or magic first must lead into the very depths of one's soul. It is only there that we can find the truths we seek. It is impossible to do this without truly understanding one's Self. This goes far beyond simply understanding why one has chosen such a path to begin with.

Although it is always wise to use caution when working with aspects of darkness, one must keep in mind that most dangers and obstacles along the way will not be from external entities or demons, or even from malicious practitioners; most obstacles will come from within: our fears, bad habits, wishful thinking, and personal demons.

Power and Darkness

In exploring the aspects of darkness, an underlying theme of power often emerges. There are some people who are drawn to dark paths, or dark themes in general, because of a feeling of powerlessness or lack of control in their lives. As a spirituality, Dark Paganism does offer a channel of self empowerment for those in tune with the darker aspects, but this is by far only a small part of its design.

Just as there will always be people attracted to Paganism in general in search of a sense of power, control, and identity, some will seek the same in Dark Paganism, maybe more so because we can admit to the desire for power.

In our culture, we have always found a fascination with darkness. The vampire myth, for example is still drawn from today so that, through the vampire, we can experience the power of lust and control over others. It is directly linked to our sexuality – often that part of it that we tend to hide.

Even in such modern tales such as *Star Wars* we are warned of how easily we can be drawn into or seduced by the "dark side"; how enticing and powerful it is. In fact, such a dark side is often equated with great power, and in Hollywood it is often the villain who has the more exciting or seductive powers. In many stories the power of "evil" is more powerful and the forces of "good" only win because the hero stops the villain from actually obtaining that power. As mentioned earlier, although darkness is not necessarily evil, it is often associated with it. Darkness has come to represent one's desire for power and thus, due to society's fear or shame of such desires, has in turn become equated with evil.

The dark side *is* empowering to many people. Darksiders get a thrill from its symbolism. Just as any magical practitioner would use candles and incense to create an atmosphere more conducive to magic work (and therefore empowering) so would a Dark Pagan use a cemetery or gothic imagery.

A true Dark Pagan can accept the reality that we sometimes feel the need for a sense of power, just as we all feel lust and anger. As humans it is our nature to feel such "dark" emotions or desires. They can motivate us and give us direction. Those with strength of will can use these carnal drives toward self-improvement and empowerment. Denying these drives robs us of our humanity and stagnates the soul.

Power *can* lead to corruption, and for a Dark Pagan, this is probably the greatest trap. However there is no shame in a desire for power, although *alone* it is a weak goal on a viable spiritual path. The application of that power, and the means by which it is achieved, is also of concern. A true practitioner of magic has a strong enough will to use such empowerment with self-control and maturity. With power comes responsibility.

There is a saying: Power corrupts, absolute power corrupts absolutely. In reality, it is not the power that corrupts – it is the person with the power who corrupts. We all have the potential to be a saint or a tyrant. Dictators were not born corrupt: they were normal children who grew up to obtain power and use it for oppression. When we are above the law we can easily convince ourselves that we mean well. Boundaries can be a tool for discipline. Darkness is not necessarily lawless and chaotic; it is, however, less restrictive. We are responsible for our actions and so with this great power comes great responsibility.

We must face the consequences of our decisions. Abusing power too much will result in our downfall and thus loss of power. By keeping ourselves in check we learn to use that power wisely and safely – to enjoy it and maintain it. The reason power corrupts is that we are conditioned to living a life of constant restraint. We don't know how to handle freedom. This is the effect of a predominantly lightside culture where one is encouraged to conform and operate under rules and protocols. When suddenly we are free of these restraints, we run amok, never having learned the art of true self-discipline. Self-discipline only begins when we make an active attempt at controlling our behavior. Being conditioned into subservience is not to be mistaken as discipline. We are "well behaved" because we are placed within a controlled environment, not because of a conscious desire to do so. Without that true discipline, once that underlying structure breaks down anarchy ensues. Order within a controlled environment is not true order – it is a poor facsimile that is not easily maintained. A sheep without its shepherd is lost; a wolf without its pack can survive. A harsh analogy indeed, but a point to remember all the same.

Ethics and the Three-fold Law

I would love to say there are no ethics in Dark Paganism and leave it at that, but that would leave many unanswered questions.

Ethics are protocols for beings that live beyond instinct into the realm of reason. This is most predominant in humans but other highly social creatures, such as the chimpanzee, have develop their own set of protocols for behavior within the collective. These protocols attempt to provide an atmosphere where we can co-exist in some level of peace. Ethics, therefore, is an aspect of *humanity*, not religion. It is a social issue, not a religious one.

"Do what thou wilt" may be the whole of the law, especially when we have no fear of divine punishment for our actions, but this in no way means we have no need to fear the consequences of our action. Obviously causing others intentional harm opens oneself to retribution by those that were harmed, and thus is probably not the wisest choice of lifestyles. Therefore, in order to protect our own interests it is wise to respect the needs of others.

Paganism is a very life-affirming spirituality by nature. Dark Paganism is no exception, despite being more attuned to the darker aspects of nature. It would not make sense for *any* Pagan to want to cause unnecessary destruction or suffering, although a Dark Pagan is more willing to accept the fact that often harm is inevitable. We live in a competitive society and so sometimes for one to gain, others must then lose.

Dark Pagans tend to be realists, and so concepts such as the Three-Fold Law of Wiccan belief need to be re-evaluated. The Three-Fold Law states that any energy sent out returns three times stronger to the sender. Therefore, "cursing" someone would, in the end, be harmful to the person who is doing the actual "cursing."

Many Dark Pagans try to rebel against the Three-Fold Law completely, believing that it is simply the remnants of Judeo-Christian thinking or a way to keep novice Pagans from misusing magic.

There is, however, some value to the Three-Fold Law. I do *not* believe there is some sort of "cosmic force" that punishes those who use magic maliciously and rewards those who strive to benefit others; the lesson of this law is far simpler.

Metaphysically speaking, when using magic in a harmful manner, the practitioner is aligning him or herself to this negative energy, making that person more receptive to physical manifestations that could be self-defeating. This is why a seasoned practitioner uses shielding and proper banishing to clear any residual negativity. In other words, done properly, there are no adverse side effects to working harmful magic in itself. Of course sometimes the effects are not as we expect. Getting what we want or think we want is not necessarily the best thing for us. Thus the need to take responsibility for our actions and accept the harsh reality that often what works well in theory fails miserably in practice. The important point is that any seemingly adverse effects of working magic were not dealt out by some external balancing force, but simply the natural process of cause and effect. It is wise to consider the consequences of *any* action, be it magical or physical.

Psychologically speaking, when performing magic of a harmful intent, the practitioner is focusing a lot of negative emotions in order to raise energy. If the person does this on a regular basis, it could lead to stress, anxiety, mental instability, etc. Of course, only an unstable person would have a desire to constantly be working harmful magic anyway!

Therefore, although there is no force that is punishing us for using magic maliciously, the Three-Fold Law does remind us of the dangers of working with destructive forces. In this same manner, working with healing forces could have positive repercussions to the practitioner, but not necessarily.

The Wiccan Rede, on the other hand, may seem like a very simple code of conduct but that is far from the case. The Rede basically says to do as one wishes as long as it harms no one. This is an extremely open and flexible statement. It requires one to be constantly aware of one's actions and of the potential repercussions of those actions. The

Rede is also very dangerous in that it relies on solely on the individual to interpret what is and is not acceptable. Those who lack the clarity or maturity to truly think things out can easily assume one's actions will harm no one when they actually do. Of course one must first determine what is to be considered "harm" and when it may or may not be justified. In this context the true complexity and demanding nature of the Rede becomes apparent. It requires great discipline to not only take responsibility for one's actions but to also face the consequences of those decisions.

Those of us raised in religions offering strict and specific laws of ethics, such as the Judeo-Christian-Islamic religions, often have a hard time adjusting to the Rede. To many the Rede is interpreted as freedom without the fear of consequences and this is simply not the case: the Rede is not a license to run amok like an undisciplined dog in a park – sooner or later someone is going to get hurt.

I am not going to attempt to delve into justifying when harmful magic could be deemed "acceptable." This is far too personal a decision. However, using magic to harm others for the sake of domination or sense of power is simply self-defeating. Such people, to be perfectly blunt, are so caught up in their lack of self-esteem that they cannot grasp how pathetic they truly are. People who find the need to wage "magical wars" tend to be hiding from their own inadequacies.

A true practitioner of magic tends to have enough maturity and self-understanding to know the difference between using magic for self-defense and using magic for self-esteem. Always remember the first law of Magic: *Know thyself.*

Dualism and Polarity

The concepts of dualism and polarity are used quite frequently in religious and magical discourse, but are rarely understood by the average practitioner today. Dualism and polarity are *not* the same, and the misunderstanding that these terms are synonymous is the primary reason for the rampant imbalance of overly "fluffy" New Age Paganism.

The term "dualism" and "duality" should not be confused. Both dualism and polarity operate within the concept of a *duality* that separates the world into two opposites. The difference between dualism and polarity is in how the opposites are viewed and how they relate to one another.

Dualism, according to *The New Grolier Multimedia Encyclopedia*, is "any theory or system of thought that recognizes two and only two independent and mutually irreducible principles or substances, which are sometimes complimentary and sometimes in conflict."

In terms of spirituality, the dualism of good and evil from the Judeo-Christian-Islamic worldview is a primary example of dualism in conflict, whereas the duality of the Goddess and God of Wiccan theology is a form of complimentary dualism[1]. However, dualism is not just used in a spiritual context. In philosophy, for example, Descartes' metaphysical dualism of mind and body, both of which are necessary to create reality, is an example of complimentary dualism.

While dualism specifically indicates a complete separation of two principles, polarity functions under the premise of one underlying whole that can be viewed as a level of degrees or balancing interaction of two poles. For example, in the Judeo-Christian-Islamic dualism of good and evil, although one may argue that something may be more evil, it does not make the lesser of the two evils any more good. Evil is independent of good; something is either good or it is evil – there is no polarity. Obviously, in terms of good or evil, one's perception may vary with others, but the division itself is *finite* per that perception of the dualism.

Polarity, on the other hand, defines each side by the other and the interaction of the two. Although there may be two poles, the underlying emphasis is on the *whole*. Polarity simply allows for various perspectives of that whole. The symbol of the yin-yang perfectly describes the nature of polarity.

---

[1] One can also justifiably argue that Wiccan theology is a monism where nature or the universe itself is a single whole and the God and Goddess are merely aspects of nature through a male/female polarity. Wiccan views on this vary, but from the perspective of deity itself, there is a female/male dualism – deity is either Goddess or God.

Each side is an aspect of a greater whole, containing a bit of the other within it.

Figure 2: The Yin-Yang

This difference is extremely important because it influences how we perceive the world. For example, the reason for the imbalance of overly fluffy New Age Lightside Paganism, especially in Wicca, is because many have attempted to incorporate the good/evil dualism of Judeo-Christian-Islamic thought into the context of polarity. This has happened because many of today's Pagans are self-taught, receiving little or no formal training[1]. The problem is that most of today's Pagans came from a Judeo-Christian-Islamic background and thus have been conditioned to view things in a dualistic manner.

Pagan paths are mystery religions. A mystery religion must be experienced in order to understand its profound teachings. Through proper study, practice and meditation, we learn to

---

[1] As mentioned earlier, formal training is not necessary assuming one has developed adequate disciplinary skills to include practice and experimentation as part of one's study. The problem is that many rely solely on books and thus don't grasp the profound yet subtle concepts underlying the belief system.

change our perception of the universe away from dualism to a more "wholistic" view. Unfortunately, this takes time and very few books have been written to cover anything more than the superficial basics. Thus, today an unfortunate majority of Paganism is composed of self-taught individuals and groups still trapped in the conflicting dualistic mindset of Judeo-Christian-Islamic conditioning. They unintentionally, and often unconsciously, split polarity into conflicting sides creating dualism when there is none. To them Wicca is "light" and therefore "good", while "dark" paths are "evil". Such a distinction was never intended to be part of Wiccan belief and certainly was not part of the craft when it first developed.

Gender vs. Polarity

This misunderstanding of polarity and association with dualism causes other problems as well, particularly with the masculine/feminine polarity. The feminine/passive – male/active polarity is based on the symbolism of the creative principle (i.e. coitus), not stereotypical gender characteristics. These attributes were not intended to define attributes of actual gender.

Assigning attributes to gender based on the masculine/feminine polarity is a generalization at best. These generalizations can lead to stereotypical thinking. Although many magical traditions like to work with polarity, common experience has proven to us that most things do not fit neatly into one category.

Gender attributes can vary with the culture. In some ancient cultures, men were hunters and women were gatherers, but in others, like the ancient Celts, the women fought right beside the men in battle. Using this polarity to define the attributes of deities is also very misleading: for any goddess there is often a god with a similar attribute and vice versa. For example, there are sun goddesses and moon gods, although they are not as common.

This may seem like common sense – a simple matter of semantics – yet it astounds me how often I see these gender stereotypes being confused with polarity. For example: I am quiet and reserved therefore I could be said to be more attuned to feminine energies... does that mean I am more woman-like because I am quiet? Does this mean that women should be more passive? Think about it.

As useful as polarity is in helping to understand the underling forces at work, it was not designed as a means of pigeonholing everything into a category. The attributes are not associative. Very few things in nature are so easily categorized. Polarity can be very useful in understanding specific aspects of nature. It helps us to understand better the interplay of energy on a metaphysical level. Unabandoned dualistic thinking influences us to use polarity as a quick means of labeling everything and we become too involved in the labeling process. Duality is simply one of many tools and was not meant to be taken literally.

It astounds me when I see arguments about whether a circle is efficient when consisting of the same sex, especially when the participants are gay or lesbian. Granted the energy may have a different "flavor" but that does not discount its effectiveness. I have been to same sex circles that were powerful and I have been to others that were not, just as I have seen in traditional mixed sex circles. Gender was not the issue. Some circles work, some don't – the factors involved are limitless. Anyone can work with polarity because that polarity is intrinsic *within* each of us, regardless of one's gender or sexual preference.

Blood, Pain, and Sacrifice

The themes of blood, pain, and sacrifice are often associated with darkness. Although one walking a dark path would be less likely to be afraid of exploring such options, these themes are by no means limited to dark paths.

Blood

It did not take long for humans to discover that the significant loss of blood for any living creature spelled its death. Such an association with the life force eventually lead to the use of blood in ritual. Blood sacrifice allowed the ancient priests of many religions to offer the life force of the offering to the deities in hopes of appeasing them. Still others hoped to directly harness and direct the life force to increase the potency of magic.

Warriors of many cultures would drink the blood or eat the heart of their enemies to capture their strength. So, too, would hunters do the same of their prey in order to absorb the power of that beast, for the blood was believed to carry the very essence of that creature.

The use of blood is considered a taboo by many modern Pagan traditions, particularly the white-light varieties, in order to counteract the stigma of blood sacrifices placed upon Pagans as a whole. However, in instances where blood is used in modern forms of Paganism, it is more commonly drawn directly from the practitioner. Traditionally, in many cultures and religions blood and wine are often interchangeable in ritual, although such a substitute would not work well with spells.

In magic, blood serves as a binding agent in spells. Magical tools can be consecrated with a drop of the practitioner's blood to bind the tools to the magician. Likewise blood can link a spell to the recipient physically, while the practitioner uses visualization to complete the link. Although a lock of hair or fingernail clipping can also be powerful binding agents, they do not have the same metaphysical connection as blood.

Apart from use as a binding agent, the use of blood, even one's own, is believed by many to infuse the working of magic with one's life energy. Blood is believed to contain our very essence. The psychological factors alone – the sense of power, mystery, and devotion one experiences in drawing and using one's own blood – can also be useful in charging the magic work.

A form of modern blood sacrifice that has been growing in popularity in the Pagan Community is through blood donations. Such an activity serves not only as an act of devotion, but as an act of compassion by helping to save lives.

Pain

Altered Consciousness through Pain

Pain is seen by many to be an act of devotion, sacrifice, and purification. It forces us to experience the moment. Through endorphins, a natural painkiller produced by our bodies, pain can induce an altered state of consciousness. Terms such as "runner's high" have been used to define the effects of endorphins on the body. In fact, many people become addicted to physical exercise due to the euphoric feelings the production of endorphins can produce. A similar state of consciousness, equated with a spiritual experience, is termed "subspace" in the BDSM[1] community.

Subspace is a transcendental-like state experienced by many submissive partners during a BDSM scene. A "scene" is the term used to define the interaction during role-playing since often the dominants and submissives behave much differently in their everyday lives. These scenes allow the participants to explore parts of their nature they typically keep locked away. In fact, the cathartic effect such interactions can produce is not unlike that of shadow integration mentioned earlier in this book. During a BDSM scene, the participants are able to acknowledge and act out these repressed feelings in an accepting environment.

---

[1] BDSM refers to the various forms of Bondage and Dominance (or Discipline), and Sadism and Masochism.

The experience of subspace varies with the individual but typically it is characterized by a sense of connection to the dominant and a feeling of surrender, not only to the dominant but also to the various internal barriers of one's conscious mind. The submissive is suddenly simply existing in the present with no trappings of identity – it is often described as "unadulterated freedom." Dominant partners can also experience a form of altered consciousness that is termed "domspace." Domspace, again varying with the individual, differs from subspace and is commonly characterized with a sense of detachment yet single-minded focus on the scene.

Light flogging or scourging can also be used to produce an altered state of consciousness. When using flogging for this purpose, the idea is not to inflict pain (although some may prefer that) but to allow its rhythmic motions to draw us into a trance-like state. As sensitivity deadens, the flogging can become harder, but this is up to the individual. The goal is not to draw blood, but to promote an altered state of consciousness for divination, visions, or prayer. Of course some individuals, particularly those involved in BDSM, may use flogging simply to have fun[1].

It is interesting to also point out that bondage equipment alone can convey a subtle yet powerful reaction even to those not directly involved in

---

[1] Keep in mind that in standard S&M most people are not using pain for mystical purposes. I am merely using examples within S&M since in using pain, such a subculture has developed a better sense of how we react to pain. The creation of terms such as "subspace" and "domspace" is a perfect example of this insight into pain.

such practices. Simply donning the regalia of a dominant can transmit subtle psychological cues to an observer who then perceived the owner as being inherently dominant. For example, someone wearing a leather outfit, spiked collar, or carrying handcuffs will be perceived as intimidating in some manner to the casual observer. For this very reason, many darksiders, particularly Satanists, use such equipment as props in their rituals since it empowers them both in instilling a sense of dominance in themselves and a sense of submissiveness in observers. Likewise, submissive gear, such as harnesses, collars, and leashes can instill a sense of submission in the wearer and a sense of dominance in the observer.

Sexual arousal increases one's threshold for pain. When we are aroused, pain is more likely to be interpreted as erotic stimulation, which is why many of us find ourselves pondering where the scratches or hickeys came from after an intense sexual encounter. Had we not been aroused, we would have sensed the scratching or biting as pain and instinctually flinched to avoid it. This also explains why many find pain pleasurable. It is not so much that they enjoy pain, but that it is interpreted as increased stimulation when they are aroused.

Rites of Passage

Throughout time, some sort of ritual pain has been included in rites of passage such as coming of age ceremonies and initiations. Although often considered to exist in more tribal cultures, such practices live on in "modern society" in the form of traditions such as fraternity hazing or playing pranks on "the new guy" at work in certain occupations. Such initiatory practices are intended to strengthen the bonds between members of a group and develop a sense of brotherhood. Unfortunately, fraternal hazing is often taken to the extreme, resulting in bitterness and resentment rather than camaraderie.

Rites of passage involving the infliction of pain come in many forms. Many cultures mark these occasions with tattoos, piercings, circumcision, or other forms of body modification. Probably the most well-known form of body modification as a right of passage is circumcision, since it is practiced by many major religions today.

Circumcision is the surgical removal of all or part of the foreskin of the human male or of the corresponding tissues of the female (clitoridectomy). Male circumcision has been widely practiced as a religious rite since ancient times. Although its origins are unknown, earliest evidence of the practice dates from ancient Egypt about 2300 BCE, where it is thought to have been used originally to mark male slaves. However, by the time of the Roman takeover of Egypt in 30 BCE, the practice had a ritual significance, and only circumcised priests could perform certain religious offices.

Circumcision and other forms of genital mutilations appear widely among tribal peoples of Africa, the Malay Archipelago, New Guinea, Australia, and the Pacific Islands as well as certain South and Central Native American groups. In tribal settings, these practices are nearly always associated with traumatic puberty rites. Sometimes the severed part is offered as a sacrifice to spirit beings. The operation certifies the subject's readiness for marriage and adulthood and testifies to his or her ability to withstand pain.

According to the Levitical law of Judaism, every Jewish male infant must be circumcised on the eighth day after birth as an initiatory rite, under penalty of ostracism from the congregation of Israel. Among the Arabs, circumcision existed before the time of Muhammad (around 570 CE). Although the Koran does not mention it, Islamic custom demands that Muslim males be circumcised before marriage (although generally performed in infancy) as a sign of spiritual purification. Some Islamic peoples practice female circumcision and the culture encourages the sexual control of women. Circumcision is absent from the Hindu-Buddhist and Confucian traditions, and in general the Christian church has no specific doctrine about it.

Although male circumcision is a simple operation, female circumcision is a more painful and debilitating procedure, which is done for aesthetic reasons and/or to reduce the female's sexual desires. This practice has been made illegal in many countries but its practice is so ingrained in these cultures that little can be done to effectively stop it. Female circumcision is viewed as a way of purifying women of their masculinity. This is because the clitoris is viewed as an undeveloped penis. A woman who still has her clitoris intact is viewed as being somewhat bisexual. The circumcised are seen as being complete women who are chaste and thus making them more suitable for marriage. Culturally, female circumcision is considered an aspect of family honor.

Tattoos, from Tahitian word meaning "to mark", are used by many people consciously or unconsciously to mark significant changes in their life. There is a sense of sacredness in choosing to accept pain in order to move into a new phase of life or connect with a stronger sense of identity. The permanence of such a ritual requires a certain level of dedication and is yet another form of symbolic sacrifice. Although many today get tattoos to be trendy, many find the act in some way spiritual. Often the artwork contains personal significance, making the act all the more meaningful.

Piercings, too, are often obtained for reasons more than fashion. For many it is a statement of non-conformity or even sexuality, while for others they mark momentous occasions. In reflecting on my own piercings I am quick to recall the reasons for each. Although some were done on a whim, most were done in response to various changes in my life.

Ear and other body piercings is seen by many teens as an informal rite of passage, as parents often will not allow piercings until a certain age. Piercings, as with tattoos and unnatural hair colors, can also mark the point where a child no longer accepts certain limitations set by parents, marking their first outright rebellious actions and thus a significant step on their path to independence. They also, consciously or not, help many teens establish themselves with their peers. Fitting in at that age is an essential drive as it allows them to develop the social skills that are often necessary to succeed later in life and even to develop healthy relationships.

Conformity, although not particularly of high interest to darksiders, is needed to some extent if one wishes to interact reasonably in society. Most older darksiders strive for a balance between their individuality and the need to integrate to some degree with society. Such compromises allow them to get a decent job and live a comfortable life that the complete social outcast would find difficult, if not impossible, to achieve. The young are fortunate enough to have the opportunity to explore their individuality far more intensely before the pressures of everyday life become a burden.

Although typically more symbolic in modern Pagan practices, especially Wiccan, there are still Pagan groups that use actual flogging during initiation. The pain is a form of sacrifice that the initiate must endure to move on to the next level. Even when the flogging is more symbolic, the fear of pain, coupled with the traditional binding of the often skyclad (nude) initiate proves to be a very powerful experience. Such a humbling experience solidifies one's commitment to the group and symbolizes the death and rebirth of the novitiate. The scourge is a symbolic ritual tool used in some Wiccan traditions such as the Alexandrian tradition.

Pain as Purification and Sacrifice

Self-flagellation can be found within many religious traditions including some Christian traditions and cultural adaptations. This form of penance or purification is the ultimate act of sacrifice, for the offering being made is oneself.

A more extreme form of self-sacrifice and purification can be seen in the Sun Dance of the Plain Indians. Still practiced today by contemporary Native Americans, the Sun Dance is a ritual involving sacrifice and supplication in order to ensure that harmony between all living beings is continued. The participants feel that since their existence relies on the continual taking from the earth, the only true way to pay homage to the earth is to sacrifice themselves back to it, thus completing the circle of life and signifying its renewal. The sacrifice of the dancers through fasting, thirst, and self-inflicted pain reflects the desire to return something of themselves to nature in exchange for past and future benefits. The dance itself symbolizes the death of the dancer.

Dancers fast and abstain from drinking during the three or four days of dancing as part of the sacrifice. Although not as common today, voluntary torture was part of the climax of the sun dance in certain tribes such as the Sioux and Cheyenne. In those cases the dancers were pierced through the breast or shoulder muscles by skewers which were tied to the center pole where they danced by pulling back until their flesh tore away. Sometimes the thongs that were inserted in the participants' bodies were attached to a varying number of buffalo skulls rather than to the center pole.

As would be expected, such an ordeal also resulted in an altered state of consciousness, where dancers often experienced visions or obtained spiritual teachings from spirits.

Sacrifice

As mentioned in the previous sections of this chapter, sacrifice comes in many forms, including the use of pain to symbolize the sacrifice of oneself. Regardless of the form, what matters is the sense of reverence and devotion behind the offering. The acts alone are meaningless without sincere intentions.

In some religions, such as Santeria, animal sacrifice is a normal and accepted practice. Although many in urbanized cultures find this offensive or frightening, the form of sacrifice must be taken into context with the culture. In the cultures where Vodun[1] and Santeria derived, for example, animals are raised for food at many households and regularly killed during preparation of the meal. Taking the life of an animal is a common occurrence. Since religion is so interwoven with the culture, ritualizing the taking of a life is not so surprising. Often the animal is consumed afterwards. When it is not, the meal itself was sacrificed. Where food can often be scarce, such a sacrifice of a food source holds great significance.

This seems out of place in more urbanized societies where we are detached from the slaughter and preparation of animals for our meat. Many don't see themselves as eating cow, for example, but rather as eating a specific cut of beef. In such a society the ritualized killing of an animal seems foreign and frightening. In the few instances where it has been accepted it hides

---

[1] Also called Sevi Lwa, or more commonly known as "Voodoo."

behind words such as "Kosher[1]" or "Halal[2]" where one can remain safely distanced from the details.

It is difficult for most Neopagans to accept animal sacrifice as a form of religious devotion. On the one hand, they must contend with the common misconception of Pagans performing sacrifices to "The Devil", and on the other hand, sacrifice is not accepted as part of their culture – many living in urbanized areas.

Of course, animal sacrifice of any sort is not part of the practice of the more common forms of Neopagan religions such as Wicca and Druidism, nor is it common among those more generic modern Pagan or nature-based spiritualties. Asatru[3] for example, recognizes that although their ancient ancestors celebrated the *blot* by feasting on an animal consecrated to the gods and then slaughtered, our modern needs and life-style are simpler today and so an offering of mead or other alcoholic beverage is sufficient. Some also celebrate through a "sacred barbecue" of meat

---

[1] The Hebrew word "Kasheir," or "Kosher," means fit or proper. When applied to food, the term indicates that an item is fit for consumption according to Jewish law. Animals and fowl must be slaughtered by a specialist, called a shochet, and then soaked and salted in accordance with Jewish law.
[2] Halal, when used in relation to food or drink in any form, means that it is permitted and fit for consumption by muslims. Animals and fowl must be slaughtered in accords with Islamic law.
[3] Asatru is the recreation of the ancient faith of the Northern Europeans. Practitioners strive for historical accuracy. Some Neo-Nazi groups have unfortunately warped this concept for their own racial purposes, which true Asatru followers neither condone nor tolerate.

bought in a store or obtained through hunting. The word blot itself is related to the Norse[1] words for "blood" and "sacrifice." The ritual consists of three parts, the hallowing or consecrating of the offering, the sharing of the offering with those present, and the libation to the gods.

Still, sacrifice takes on many more subtle forms from Catholics not eating meat on Fridays to Wiccans making a libation of food and drink to the Goddess and God. Many Eastern religions leave fruit and grain as offerings to both the gods and to ancestors. Fasting is a form of sacrifice and purification used by many religions and spiritual traditions. The simple act of consciously changing one's common routine in honor or recognition of the deities is a powerful expression of devotion.

---

[1] Germanic and Scandinavian.

.

Dark Spirituality

In order to understand the concept of "dark spirituality" we need to step back and begin with the basic question, *what is spirituality?* This is not something we can easily answer since the concept itself is vague and subjective. If we were to summarize this concept in a reasonably acceptable and politically correct definition we could say that spirituality is a journey – a quest – for understanding or meaning. The object of understanding itself is not always directly known but is often verbalized as being the meaning of life, the universe, or Self.

A Model of Spirituality

For us to seek out this meaning we need to start with a foundation. This foundation is our worldview, our paradigm – how we perceive and interpret the universe and our experiences. We are a very complex, multifaceted species with an intelligence that offers us limitless possibilities of ideas and perceptions, yet this vast potential is crammed into a body that in essence confines our perception into a box consisting of the five senses plus what is often referred to as intuition[1]. Our senses can only help us understand so much and the constant barrage of external stimuli of daily life often drowns the voice of our intuition out. This search for meaning therefore is based upon, and operates within, our overall perception of the universe as most commonly seen through our worldview and culture.

Although there are many cultures and perceptions, they all can be categorized into one of two schools of thought or approaches to spirituality. One school attempts to find meaning *internally* while the other school attempts to find meaning *externally*. Both are viable approaches and neither is mutually exclusive of the other; they are aspects of the singularity known as "spirituality".

---

[1] Many prefer to refer to this as the "sixth sense." The choice is purely one of semantics. Either refers to our ability to sometimes sense something that may not have any physical indications, such as hidden feelings, thoughts, and potential future events.

Figure 3: Two Approaches to Spirituality.

The external approach is popular in western culture and is based upon a dualistic mindset. The worldview of such an approach typically attempts to break down the universe and our experiences into categories in an attempt to find meaning. Our perceptions are viewed in an analytical manner. The primary question asked is *what is the meaning of the universe?* We attempt to find this meaning by understanding how it works. Some of the common characteristics in an external approach to spirituality include an emphasis on deity and doctrine as we attempt to establish an (external) focus and guidelines that are to be followed in order to reach a level of understanding. Religions adhering to this approach tend to be more structured and dogmatic as they present specific rules and guidelines toward achieving a spiritual life. These religions are geared towards the masses, grouping people together into a common framework. Those who take an external approach to spirituality like to separate things into dualisms such as good and evil. Examples of religions operating within an external approach to spirituality include Christianity, Judaism, Islam, Confucianism, and (usually) Wicca.

The internal approach to spirituality, on the other hand, is based on a mindset geared towards monism[1], thus dealing in concepts of polarity where the universe is not seen as a collection of separate independent parts, but rather as a whole consisting of many interactions and perspectives. Our perceptions are more intuitive than analytical and so the primary question is not so much a question of the meaning of the universe but more specifically *who am I? How do I fit into all this?* We attempt to find meaning by understanding how we relate to the universe and how the universe relates to us. Since the focus in this approach is based more on our personal relationship and experience with the universe, emphasis is primarily on the Self – on a search for identity and self-expression. Religions adhering to such an approach are more personalized and thus less structured. In fact, it is harder to list actual religions within this approach because such internal paths by their very nature are too personalized to be easily categorized. These religions rarely dictate specific guidelines, but rather assume the individual will discover a personal path through meditation or other practices that promote self-awareness. Examples of religions operating within an internal approach to spirituality include Taoism, modern religious

---

[1] Note: "monism" does not necessarily mean *monotheistic,* although of course monotheism is an example of monism of deity. Monism is the philosophic doctrine that ultimate reality is entirely of one substance.

Satanism, and the various forms of Dark Paganism.

Religions serve as paths towards one of these approaches, offering us techniques and symbolism to aid us in our quest for understanding. Religions are a means to *utilize* an approach, and are not themselves an approach as many insist. Fundamentalism is the result of an over emphasis on a religion – the *construct* – rather than the actual spiritual journey.

Keep in mind that the imagery associated with darkness may or may not play a role in dark spirituality. Since the same people who find dark imagery attractive will also be attracted to dark spiritual paths, there is often an overlap.

When we are raised in a culture and/or religion based upon one school of spirituality, we need to undergo a *paradigm shift* – a transformation where we experience a drastic change in our worldview – in order for us to follow paths leading to the other school. This paradigm shift allows us to perceive the paths to that school and the school itself in the proper context. Without this paradigm shift one interprets the symbolism of the paths of the other school within the context of the present one. This causes an incomplete view of the other school. Such a clash of context could be expressed as a form of culture shock. When someone experiences a culture that is different from one's own for the first time, its customs can appear strange and foreign. We cannot make sense of this new culture since it does not operate within the framework of what we are accustomed to in our own culture. It is only when we learn to understand the culture from its own perspective and history that we are better able to appreciate it.

For a paradigm shift to occur one must actively practice in that path's construct since a spiritual path must be experienced, not learned. Through symbolism, ritual, and practice we eventually find a personal connection to that path/religion at which point it becomes a part of us. This is the true internal initiation that the initiation rite metaphorically represents.

Up until now I have been taking a dualistic approach to this model of spirituality in order to better separate and explore the two schools/approaches to spirituality. Although this approach works well on paper, in the real world living spiritual paths and religions do not always fall neatly into one school. There are not really two "forms" of spirituality – simply two general approaches to expressing and working with one's spirituality.

In practice, any given path will have a leaning or disposition toward one school, but will still contain some elements of the other. Therefore, the model of spirituality outlined above works more on the basis of polarity. Some religions such as Christianity are very structured with clearly defined laws (in this case the Ten Commandments). There is no question as to which school of spirituality it belongs since it is clearly external in nature. Pagan/neo-pagan paths are less structured and intentionally open to interpretation, thus are more likely to be used within either school. For example, Wicca is most commonly practiced within the construct of the external/light approach. This is especially evident in the area of ethics where there are such guidelines as the Wiccan Rede and the Three-fold Law. Granted, these laws are not as specific as the Ten Commandments of Christianity, but there is a strong emphasis on them all the same.

Any religion or spiritual path, however, could be practiced within the context of the other approach to spirituality. Pagan paths work well within the context of either school because they are relatively unstructured religions. Religions that are more extreme in one approach, such as Christianity, can also be adapted to work in the other school, but not as easily. In this case, any given *religion* in the Christian faith would be difficult to incorporate into the other school, but the *spirituality* of Christianity could be adapted quite well. Keep in mind that religions are designed to work within a specific school and thus designed around that approach, while general spirituality can be utilized by either.

There are many paths all leading to the same goal. For example, Christian symbolism and myth can be quite powerful and fulfilling when practiced within an internal/dark context. It all depends on what works best for each individual. This is an important point: the various organized religions of the world are tools to assist one in reaching a spiritual life – they are not the end in themselves. As mentioned earlier, Fundamentalists have reversed the focus away from a more encompassing sense of spirituality back into the construct itself; the *religion* has become the goal. Such an imbalance and misdirection of focus manifests though the claim of "one true faith."

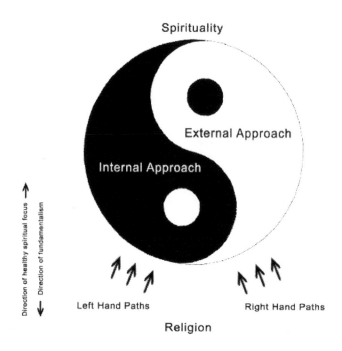

Figure 4: Model of Spirituality

This *Religious spirituality* could be considered a general view of spirituality based upon the imagery of a specific religion or tradition. It is the general goal and sense of self that these religions wish to obtain and the areas of spirituality one's paradigm chooses to focus on. It is spirituality as seen from the perspective of one's paradigm. In Christianity it could be a sense of humility and peace – of being loved by a great paternal deity and being accepted by this deity unconditionally. In Wicca it is a sense of connection both to the God and Goddess as well as a connection to nature.

Religion itself is not necessary on a spiritual journey, but it can be a useful tool. It provides the groundwork and imagery to assist one in understanding, or at least addressing, the mysteries of the universe, and have survived the test of time.

Now that we have a working model of spirituality, we can explore the paths or religions leading to spirituality.

What Makes a Path Dark?

Before defining a dark path (or left-hand path[1]) it would help to first define a light, or right-hand, path. A light path is aligned with the active /masculine[2]/ yang/logical aspects of the universe and human nature. These paths work with external frames of reference, such as dogma or specific codes of ethics and morality. The paths themselves dictate the way its adherents should act. Besides the Judeo-Christian-Islamic religions of the West and Confucianism of the East, most

---

[1] Whether or not "dark path" and "left hand path" should be used synonymously is debatable among some darksiders. Most of the fair arguments I have heard attempt to define a left hand path as a subset of the various religions and philosophies that would fall under the category of a dark path. In this case, a left hand path would be considered a dark path lacking religious trappings. A left hand path would then be considered purely a religion of the self, lacking any true deity other than the self. Apart from this technicality, both paths share the same attributes discussed in the definition of a dark path in this chapter. The distinction, if any, is left up to the reader.

[2] Don't confuse the male/female aspects of polarity with gender stereotypes. The terminology here is intended to help one better understand the interplay of energy on a metaphysical level only.

Neopagan religions such as Wicca fall under this category. These Pagan religions, although less dogmatic, still specify a particular code of ethics. The Wiccan Rede and the Three-Fold Law, for example, although being more flexible and open to interpretation, are still external codes to which practitioners are expected to adhere. A right-hand path religion also has a tendency towards submission or supplication to an external force, be it a deity, nature, or creation itself; we are often considered below deity in some respect.

A dark path is attuned with the passive/feminine/ yin/intuitive aspects of the universe and human nature. Such paths are more individualistic and less structured than light paths. There are no set moral codes or ethics. Followers of a dark path are more aware of and take responsibility for their actions, both physically and in regards to magic. Blame for our woes is not placed on "the devil" or "bad karma" but on the consequences of our choices and, of course, on pure chance for those things we simply cannot control. Dark paths are focused on the Self. Deities may or may not play a role in their practice.

Left-hand paths stress the transcendence of our limitations to become all that we can possibly be in *this* life. Attributes such as strength and pride, which are sometimes viewed as "corrupt" or "evil" or in some way out of balance in a right-hand path, are embraced with passion on the dark paths.

A right-hand path stresses transcendence of self to a higher, more spiritual form. Often this is an externalized goal, such as something reached in an afterlife. There is an emphasis on seeking "oneness" with the universe or deity where individuality is deemed an illusion to be shed in the process. Left-hand paths, on the other hand, emphasize a separation from this unity, empowering individuality. When a dark path does emphasize a sense of connection or unity, it is done in a way that still acknowledges the individual. Taoists, for example, wish to be one with the Tao, but in doing so they strive to be one with themselves and to act spontaneously according to their nature. There is no external means of becoming one with the Tao; it can only be found from within.

While many right-hand paths have a tendency to operate under the precept of opposing or aggressive dualism, separating these yin/yang polarities into opposing forces, left-hand paths view the universe as the interaction of polarities within the construct of one unifying whole. It is only when nature or the individual incorporates both sides of the dark/light polarity rather than impose one side over the other, that balance is achieved; to shun all aspects of its opposite is to invite disaster.

Balance does not necessarily mean "equal," but rather that a healthy, viable interaction of the two forces is being maintained. Balance is *relative*, not absolute. Therefore, either a right-hand path or a left-hand path can be balanced in itself with a natural predisposition towards either dark (internal) or light (external) themes. What we see with the growing popularity of the new-age movement is a general loss of balance among many of the light side paths of Paganism where darkness has been mistakenly associated with evil. Those following a dark spiritual path or lifestyle struggle openly with the often powerful pull of their "darker side", believing it better to confront their fears and challenges rather than ignore or hide them in shame or self delusion. There is no shame in accepting one's humanity and all the baggage that comes with it. Being human is not easy.

Right-hand path religions are more common since they are in essence simpler. By submitting to the tenets of that path in a form of herd-mentality, one can live securely in the belief that they are on the road to spiritual bliss, if not in this lifetime, then in the next life or afterlife. Right-hand paths are religions for the common people, for the masses – those who don't wish to dance to the beat of their own drum. Although some on the darker paths may discount the potential for spiritual growth on such a path, many do in fact find light paths spiritually fulfilling. *Any* path is valid in its own right, but not necessarily the best path for everyone.

Dark paths are by their very nature more difficult and thus less popular since the practitioner must define or construct his or her own path to enlightenment and wholeness. The idea of relying solely on oneself for spiritual growth and enlightenment is a frightening concept to the average person. Although this seems elitist, it is basic fact: it takes a certain type of individual with a strong sense of character to be drawn to, and navigate within, a dark path.

Since such individuals have less of a need for organized religions to justify their beliefs, there are fewer examples of specific religions geared towards a dark path. The more well-known spiritual paths to fall under the category of a dark path, or left-hand path, such as Taoism, Satanism, and various forms of Dark Paganism will be discussed later in this chapter. However, many examples of dark paths are highly individualized personal paths that defy simple categorization. Such dark paths may have different constructs and symbolism, but tend to share certain universal traits that define a path as a "dark path."

In exploring the general concepts of a dark path, one discovers many underlying tenets. They are often not directly expressed, but more likely simply assumed or expressed through the general attitude of the practitioners.

Assumed Universal Tenets of a Dark Path

- Darkness is simply the natural complement to light and not necessarily bad or "evil."

- We all have within us a "dark side." Many ignore it, but we cannot escape it for it *is* a part of us.

- The path to spiritual enlightenment is through understanding of the Self.

- One cannot truly know the Self without first accepting and embracing our "dark side."

- Although we may seek others of like mind to share our experiences, all paths to enlightenment are by nature solitary paths and thus very personal. We may benefit and learn from others, but in the end, we alone must complete our journey. (Asking for help is not a sign of weakness; depending upon it is.)

- One's religious beliefs and deities are merely tools for self-expression and understanding. They can be useful tools, but are not necessary. Whether or not deities truly exist is inconsequential.

- Enlightenment is a growing process, not a goal to be reached. It is endless, and perhaps never completely attainable.

- On the path to enlightenment, the journey is more important than the destination. It should enhance the quality of one's life, not restrict it. Life should be enjoyed, not sacrificed.

Although many who walk the various dark paths tend to have a certain fascination with death, it is more its symbolism that is found to be intriguing. Most are not concerned with the ideas of an afterlife. It may seem ironic that dark paths are more centered on life than death. To the sojourner of a dark path, life should be lived fully and enjoyed – it should be experienced. Instead of brooding over "should have" and "could have" they simply DO. We should take risks when appropriate and learn from our mistakes, always accepting responsibility for our actions.

Death is inevitable, and those who walk on dark paths accept that it is also a great uncertainty. We may like to think that there is an afterlife, and may even entertain certain beliefs as to what happens after death, but our concern is on the here and how. It is pointless to focus too much energy on something we can neither understand nor control.

There are various forms a dark path can take. Some may simply be attuned to deities of a darker nature, while others may radically chastise the shallowness and ignorance of many "light-side" paths. Some wear black and gothic jewelry; others do not stand out in a crowd. The true distinction between a light path and a dark path is *internal*. It is an attitude and a paradigm. It is very personal.

Dark Paganism

Of the various dark path religions, Dark Paganism is the most encompassing. It is important to understand that Dark Paganism is not a specific tradition or group of traditions, but rather an inner disposition of certain Pagans who may adhere to any given tradition or form of Paganism. Simply put, Dark Paganism consists of any Pagans who are personally attuned to the darker aspects of nature, tending to be attracted to deities of a darker caliber. It is a relatively new path that arose from the overlap of the various dark lifestyles and Paganism. Such individuals were displeased with the steady infiltration of fluffy New Age attitudes in mainstream Paganism which equated darkness with evil and thus began to form their own approaches to Paganism centered around their own imagery and attitude.

Due to the very individualistic nature of any dark path, Dark Pagans are commonly solitary and eclectic in design. Instead of simply worshipping dark deities, Dark Pagans seek a personal connection with them. Ritual form is typically the same as is found in Lightside Paganism, although they are often adapted to include darker imagery to personalize them to the practitioner's tastes.

As with other dark paths, dark paganism emphasizes self-exploration and self-expression more so than mainstream paganism. Those with Wiccan backgrounds seek to revive Wicca's original stance that darkness is but the natural complement to light and not necessarily bad or evil. Both light and dark offer their own wisdom and gifts, neither of which should be overlooked.

Although terms such as "the shadow" of Jungian psychology may not be known or utilized by all Dark Pagans, all would recognize that being human means that we are not perfect. They recognize that they have a dark side and have chosen to take ownership of it in order to better themselves or to at least better understand who they are.

While some Dark Pagans view their personal paths as a way of counteracting the imbalance of overly white-light Pagan paths in an effort to reclaim Paganism from dulling new-age influences, many others have simply drifted away from any associations with their roots.

Taoism

At first glance, Taoism may not appear to be a dark path since it lacks the dark imagery often associated with the more notable dark paths of Western culture. However, the underlying principles of Taoism are by their very nature aligned with the principles of other dark paths, although often more eloquently presented. Despite Taoism's focus on balance as a spiritual path/life philosophy, it still uses the internal approach to spirituality mentioned earlier in this chapter.

Taoism has developed into several forms, the most marked distinction being between the philosophical and religious manifestations.

Religious Taoism

The goal of the religious stream of Taoism, known as *Tao-chiao*, is in the attainment of immortality, be it physical or spiritual, which can be achieved through alchemy. Taoist alchemy itself has two forms, outer alchemy (*wai-tan*) and inner alchemy (*nei-tan*). Outer alchemy is a physical form of alchemy and is believed to be the older of the two. In essence, it is not unlike the alchemy of the West. Inner alchemy, which is more prevalent today, is a metaphoric alchemy that makes use of a combination of meditative breathing and sexual techniques to strengthen, control, and direct the flow of *chi* (vital energy) throughout the body. The use of dietary practices, fasting, talismans, and teachings of philosophical Taoism are also incorporated into religious practice.

Philosophical Taoism

Instead of focusing on the attainment of physical immortality, philosophical Taoism, or *Tao-chia*, concentrates on becoming one with the Tao. The Tao itself is beyond words, but can be generally understood as *the way of things* – the unity that underlies plurality and gives life its momentum. The more one tries to define the Tao, the further one drifts from it.

Through meditation and observing nature, the Taoist seeks to achieve an internal balance and learn to "act with out acting," known as *wu-wei*. This concept of inaction is very misunderstood by most Westerners since it appears to lack a competitive edge. However the concept of "going with the flow", vs. going against it, has much stronger implications. The Taoist hopes to achieve a level of spontaneous action that is in accord with one's nature and not the result of personal prejudices or misdirected motivations. Non-action is not idleness, but rather knowing instinctually when to use force and when to be passive. For example, an animal will not attack unless provoked because it works naturally with the principle of *wu-wei*. Should that animal become cornered, the results can be quite forceful if not vicious.

Probably the most basic principle of Taoism is in the relativity of all things. To the Taoist, there is no ultimate or absolute attribute: all things are defined by their opposites where they blend and contrast to achieve balance and definition.

Taoism as a Dark Path

Taoism is a very internal path and as with any dark path, ethics is an internal balance, not an external creed. There are no distinct concepts of "good" and "evil", and morality is replaced with the observation of personal responsibility and cause and effect. The Taoist does not attempt to change the world, but simply seeks to harmonize with (not worship) the Tao, and in so doing seeks to live up to one's full potential and nature. As Lao Tzu, the supposed founder of Taoism, wrote: "Do nothing, but leave nothing undone." The Taoist seeks to walk his or her own path and not be swayed by the demands or expectations of others, hoping to find freedom from all forms of social conditioning.

As a very realistic path, Taoism teaches us to know – and accept – one's limitations. However, such limitations are not static and pre-ordained. The Taoist view of fate itself is very fluid. Our limitations and thus our fate are created by the interactions of our decisions and our opportunities. At any given moment, we can neither transcend them nor view them as permanent boundaries. Thus our fate constantly changes, yet always influences the current course of our lives.

Many Western interpretations of a Taoist consist of a slow moving, quiet, and overall boring individual. Although a Taoist can appreciate stillness and silence, the true Taoist is a very passionate person. Through self-understanding the Taoist seeks to come to terms with one's humanity and all that it encompasses. In striving for balance, the Taoist understands the importance of the full range of emotions be they light or dark, and is not afraid to experience and express them.

Concepts of the shadow are not new to Taoism. Long before Jung the Taoists taught that if we are to be whole and follow the way of nature we must pursue the difficult process of embracing the opposites within us. They warned against resolving the tension of our opposites by identifying with only one side, such as by attempting to be masculine and not feminine or creative and not destructive. Such a one-sided development will lead only to imbalance and thus physical or mental illness. We must seek to become a whole individual or live bitter, dissatisfied lives stripped of precious parts of our personalities.

Satanism[1]

Satanism and Dark Paganism are often confused; the subject of their similarities is frequently debated even among Satanists. However, as a spiritual path Satanism and Dark Paganism are very different. This chapter is not intended to distance Dark Paganism from its dark sibling, Satanism, but to examine how another path has developed out of darkness.

Satanism is not easy to define because there is not one generic form to use as reference. Also, as would be expected from a dark path, the views of Satanism will vary even among Satanists. Despite this, there are certain classifications that can better explain the types of Satanism that exist.

Gothic[2] Satanism

Before exploring modern Satanism, it is important to understand that it is not the same Satanism that the Christian Church invented in the 15th century as the invisible enemy, giving rise to what

---

[1] I do not intend to speak for all Satanists but rather hope to break many of the common misconceptions that run rampant even in the Pagan community. This section is based primarily on the most common generalizations made by Satanists on the subject.

[2] The use of the word "Gothic" in this respect refers to the time period and not the "gothic subculture" of modern times, which style and music centers around dark imagery. Because of their morbid or "spooky" appearance, Goths, as adherents are called, are often mistaken as "Satanists" by the ignorant.

is commonly referred to as the *Burning Times*[1]. Gothic Satanism, as this fictitious religion is referred to today, was the product of the collective shadow projection by a religion that, at the time, believed even evil thoughts were a sin. (The more we attempt to repress our dark nature, the more we will see it exaggerated in others. See chapter on *The Shadow*.) This form of Satanism never really existed, although it became a useful scapegoat to the guilt-ridden as well as a dangerous political tool for ridding oneself of one's enemies, not to mention a means of keeping the Church in power.

Gothic Satanism still lives on today in the minds of some Americans and Europeans who believe that a highly organized, international secret network of Satanists exists. This organization is said to perform rituals containing human sacrifice and sexual abuse, often involving minors, although there has yet to be a single documented case proving the existence of such an organization. Sadly, there have been localized instances of people attempting to enact such practices due to either psychosis or ignorance.

Juvenile/Exploratory Satanism and Fantasy

Due to the negative, yet often-empowering images of Satanism, many rebellious individuals (often teens) become intrigued with Satanism and practice warped and often completely fictitious versions of it. These individuals use this pseudo-Satanism as an outlet for their sexual frustrations

---

[1] Most witches were actually killed in ways other than burning, but this has become the most popular way of referring to the time of witch persecutions.

and feelings of loneliness or emotional inadequacy. Ironically, many own copies of Anton LaVey's *Satanic Bible*, yet perform animal sacrifices, a subject the book, a work of modern-day religious Satanism, does not condone at all. These same people are prone to misuse Dark Paganism or other dark paths or lifestyles in the same manner. It is very unfortunate that it is such people who tend to catch the public's eye, fueling further misunderstanding.

Modern (Religious) Satanism

Modern religious Satanism can vary greatly among its practitioners and there is no universally accepted system of beliefs or scripture. Some border on forms of Paganism while others are steadfast atheists. In fact, as ironic as it may seem, a great majority of Satanists do not actually worship Satan at all. There are also many differences in how Satanism is practiced in the United States and in Europe.

Since it would be difficult for a book, let alone this chapter, to account for all the various forms of modern religious Satanism, only two very general perspectives will be explored: theistic and atheistic Satanisms. The differences, as you will see, lie not in the way the constituents view the world, but in how they relate the concept of deity to that path.

Theistic Satanism, such Luciferianism, tends to honor certain dark deities such as Lucifer, Set, and Satan. Some variations may border on or be considered Pagan in nature, depending on how one wishes to define Paganism, or may eclectically incorporate other Pagan traditions into their Satanic framework.

Some theistic Satanists, such as devotees to specific dark deities, have developed their personal spirituality to such an extent that the determining factor in distinguishing them from the more generic term "Dark Pagan" lies purely in semantics. Also, some of these Satanists, including many Setians (members of the Temple of Set), prefer to disassociate themselves from the term "Satanist" completely, while others prefer such a categorization.

Atheistic Satanism, such as the Church of Satan, does not believe in the existence of supernatural beings such as God or the Devil and is quick to deny any associations with Paganism. To these Satanists, deities are the fictional and mythological invention of humans to help them cope with the often overwhelming mysteries of life. The Satanist is his or her own deity. Satan is usually seen as a principle or force of nature – the dark evolutionary force of entropy that permeates all of nature, providing the drive for survival. Devil worship is looked upon as being a Christian heresy and thus is frowned upon since it acknowledges the Christian view of God vs. the Devil. In order to blaspheme the Christian god, one must first accept its reality – something a Satanist would not do.

Regardless of the form of Satanism, their concept of Satan is pre-Christian, and derived from earlier pagan images of power, virility, sexuality, and sensuality. Needless to say, the Satan of Satanism holds little resemblance to the Satan of Christianity. Satanists blame much of the violence in the world on the suppression of natural behavior, such as indulgence in carnal pleasure, which the major religions, particularly Christianity, deem sinful. All forms of modern religious Satanism attempt to break free from the themes of guilt and self-sacrifice that Christianity has been known to over-emphasize, often hypocritically.

Satanists in general promote hedonism, but not to the extent of self-destruction. In fact, as a spiritual path, Satanists prioritize the self and promote practices that improve one's life, a trait common among dark paths. They strive to achieve god-hood, which is deemed the apex of human potential.

Satanism vs. Dark Paganism

Many Satanists believe that Dark Paganism is a watered-down or rehashed form of theistic Satanism where adherents are simply afraid to use the word "Satan" due to lingering Judeo-Christian-Islamic conditioning. For some this is no doubt the case, but for most, Dark Paganism is a path of its own. Satanism and Dark Paganism, although completely different religions, share similar attitudes on many topics, such as their views on shame and ethics. Both paths attempt to break free of the debilitating feelings of shame to better explore who we truly are and encourage the acceptance of our faults and weaknesses as tools towards self-improvement. This attitude is naturally common among those who follow a dark spiritual path, *regardless* of their religion.

Apart from differences in religious practice, the most important difference is in self-determination.

Satanists reserve the right to label themselves and others according to their own views of what Satanism is. Dark Pagans have neither the need nor the desire for such an association with Satanism.

Satanists generally consider themselves each their own deity, and view their birthday as a religious holiday. Most Dark Pagans don't tend to take this stance, at least not to this extreme. Also, Satanists typically prefer to move counter sunwise (widdershins) in their ritual to symbolize the forces of entropy. While some Dark Pagans also use such symbolic gestures, at least at certain times, most still move in the traditional sunwise (deosil) direction. This is partly because most Dark Pagans evolved from the more mainstream Pagan traditions and so have kept this ritual habit. The direction itself is of little consequence in ritual; its significance lies in what it means to the practitioner[1]. Additionally, while Satanists tend to be aggressive in counter-measuring all lightside approaches, Dark Pagans are typically more concerned with promoting balance among Paganism as a whole and so are not as quick to cast away all aspects of their lightside siblings.

---

[1] Many will disagree with this, stating that working in the opposite direction is bad luck or will in some way hinder the flow of magick. The fact is, we really don't know for sure if it is the direction itself or the collective associations that have been placed on those directions that matter most. The original associations were based upon the cycles observed in nature, particularly the movement of the sun. By moving in the same direction we connect unconsciously with the flow of natural energy. This, at least, is the theory, but again, it is not the *direction* but the associations we have with the direction that take precedence.

Although Satanists are considered elitist even among themselves, many Dark Pagans feel that such an elitists' attitude is a sign of imbalance. However, although elitism can indeed have its negative side, it can also be a powerful motivational tool. Since Satanists also find false or exaggerated pride to be a prelude to failure, I must remind Pagans not to fall into the trap of labeling such attributes as elitism as intrinsically negative. Raising oneself above others in a quest for self-actualization is a powerful way of breaking free from the social conditionings that can impede the process. It is a simple fact of nature that all humans were *not* created equal. Some are stronger or smarter than others. Some will never amount to more than dishwashers while others will achieve great wealth. Sometimes these limitations are circumstantial (education, wealth), but sometimes they are genetic (intelligence, health). We were not all dealt a fair hand in the game of genetics – and this has *nothing* to do with race, sexual preference, or any other label apart from the threat of prejudices. In many ways Satanism, in its stern rejection of lightside values, is often better able to cope with many darker emotions and characteristics, while Dark Pagans, typically incorporating a structure derived from lightside sources, need to tempter themselves accordingly. Dark Pagans need to be cautious not to fall into the trapping of becoming hypocritical with light-side conditioning. Satanists advocate the intensification or encouragement of the ego, often more so than the average Dark Pagan.

Despite their different approaches, all those who walk a dark path try to avoid being caught up in the "herd mentality" of the general public, hoping to find their own truths along the way. They are not quick to blindly accept spiritual doctrine, and treasure individualism above all things.

"Dark" Deities

The dark deities represent many of the same forces as any deity, but in a more raw or intense form and so are less tame or predictable. They are closer to the primal forces that drive us. Instead of deities of love, we have deities of passion and desire; instead of deities of intelligence, we have deities of wisdom and hidden knowledge.

They are the knowable, yet the unknowable – the deities to whom we find we are the closest, yet are unable to fully understand. They lurk in the shadows, the mysterious realm just outside the reach of the light of understanding.

Perhaps this closeness is why they are feared and often deemed dangerous, for that closeness to us is a threat to our false sense of security. We are inherently afraid to learn such mysteries in that they threaten to expose our weaknesses and our innermost Selves. Who knows what lurks in the darkest recesses of our own mind?

As mentioned in the Chapter *"Understanding Darkness"*, to understand the aspects of darkness it is useful to categorize these aspects into two areas: passive and active. The passive aspects are more in touch with the spiritual/intangible, whereas the active aspects are more in touch with the physical/tangible.

In studying many of the deities that would be linked to Dark Paganism, it is quite common to want to associate the aspects of the dark goddesses with the passive aspects of darkness and the aspects of the dark gods, with the active[1]. This may work with the more generic concepts of the Goddess and God, but there will always be deities that will refuse to fit neatly into any category. Keep in mind that these categories are meant to aid in the exploration of the roles of the deities and not as a means to restrict their interpretation.

The darker deities teach us that nature is not always peaceful and nurturing, and that some of the more primeval forces that drive us do not necessarily have – or need to have – redeeming qualities. Throughout history, these deities have perhaps been worshiped as a way of accepting and acknowledging the harsh – often cruel – forces they personify. These forces are just as necessary and just as sacred as the gentler, more nurturing forces to which we tend to cling for a sense of security.

Despite having a framework to provide a more balanced outlook on nature, many Neopagans have chosen to ignore the darker deities, often

---

[1] Active/passive aspects of darkness were discussed in the chapter "Understanding Darkness."

labeling them as being too chaotic or dangerous to work with. Just as we repress our "dark side" into our shadow, so too do many well-meaning, but all the same confused, Lightside Pagans repress the dark side of the deities in order to make them more appealing. Those that cannot be watered down, such as Loki, are labeled evil or dangerous and thus avoided.

It is true that many of the forces behind these deities are of a harsher, more primeval, form; but the danger lies not in these forces but in the individual's inability to handle them, either due to fear or mental instability. Obviously, these deities are not for everyone, but to not acknowledge them is to invite ignorance and lack of balance. Many of these deities *should* be feared – and even those who have embraced them know that there are boundaries that should be kept.

While some Dark Pagans adhere to specific deities, others worship a more generic goddess and god. A very common generic form of the Dark Goddess is the crone aspect of the Triple Goddess – She who has already been the Maiden and Mother and is now wise from her life experiences. The Crone has seen her share of death and has accepted Her own fate that old age brings (symbolic death in the case of a deity, where she is reborn as the Maiden again). Many fear the Crone because she reminds us of their own mortality and because she harbors many secrets in the art of magic. Her very presence instills a certain amount of fear to those who do not find comfort in her dark embrace for the Crone reigns over the destruction that precedes creation.

Many "fluffy" Pagans see her as a hag or as being too spooky to approach, but on the contrary, those who take the time to know her find that she is often smiling back at us behind that veil of darkness and mystery[1]. She is like the grandmother that can comfort a child. She is the one who truly understands our pain and suffering because in her long life she has experienced it all a thousand times. The Crone may be a goddess of death, but her spirit is very much alive.

For the Dark God, a very common generic aspect is the Horned God – He who is wild and untamable. The Horned God by his very nature is more carnal. His aspects include passion and desire – raw sexual energy. He has no shame for his passion or the erection with which he is often portrayed.

As with any form of Paganism, one does not *decide* on a goddess and god to worship, but rather *finds* them. By listing some of the deities that could be considered "dark" I am by no means suggesting that those who consider themselves Dark Pagans are limited to these deities: I am merely listing a few to help explain the underlying aspects of Dark Paganism. Naturally, those who find their calling in the darkness are more likely to be receptive to deities with darker aspects, although this is by no means necessary. *Any* deity can have darker aspects so such labels as "dark" and "light" should not be given too much weight. One's personal associations and interactions with their energy are of the greatest importance.

Below are some of the manifestations of the dark deities. Keep in mind that often deities will have

---

[1] This no doubt sounds hypocritically "fluffy", but my point is that the Crone is more approachable than she is given credit for.

more than one attribute, and may fit in more than one category, including some that are not necessarily "dark." This is even more so with the Greek deities, whose associations have been known to vary through time and even between the ancient Greek cities.

Deity as Warrior or Hunter

Typically deities of war do not engage in armed conflict themselves but use magic to aid allies and hinder foes. The goddesses associated with war, especially in Celtic traditions, were also closely associated with sexuality, being seen as both the takers and givers of life.

<u>Gwynn ap Nudd</u>: (Welsh) Appears fleetingly in Welsh folklore as a magic warrior-huntsman and as king of the fairies or lord of the underworld. Often portrayed wearing a gray cloak and riding upon a pale horse, he would set out on wild hunts to find and collect the spirits of the dead. Gwynn ap Nudd is associated with the English god Herne.

<u>Macha</u>: (Celtic, "Battle") Often confused as being a part of the triad known as The Morrigan, Macha is actually a separate triple goddess. Like The Morrigan, Macha is a goddess of war. However, she is also a goddess of childbearing and sexuality as well as a goddess of horses. Celtic women had equal status with men, and would fight side by side them. Macha is an excellent representative of the strength of those women.

According to Celtic literature, Macha's husband wagered that she could run faster than the horses of the high king in Ulster. The king then challenged him to prove his claim. In order to save her husband, Macha, who was pregnant at the time with twins, ran the race and won. As retribution for being forced to run in her condition, Macha cursed the fighting men of the north to suffer menstrual pains for "nine times nine" generations when preparing for battle.

Morrigan/Morrigu: (Celtic, "Ghost Queen", "Great Queen") Goddess of battle who was probably a pre-Celtic moon goddess. She is also seen as a goddess of death. In the form of a triple goddess, known as "The Morrigan", Morrigan combines with Badb ("scald-crow") and Nemhain ("Frenzy") and were probably manifestations of the same deity and were frequently identified with one another. Badb, or Badhbh, was not only a battle goddess, but also married to Net, a war god. These Goddesses were aspects of the single principle of war and often appeared as ravens, birds of ill omen, before and during battle in Celtic folklore.

Like many goddesses, Morrigan was able to change shape into a raven or hooded crow as well as a gray wolf and a hornless red heifer. In her manifestation as "Washer of the Ford", Morrigan appears as a woman washing bloody clothing in a river before a battle. It is a very bad omen to warriors who meet this image. In modern times, the appearance of the "Washer of the Ford" foretells of a death in the family. The double association of the river and the raven possibly suggests a link to Nantosuelia, a Gaulish river goddess, who was also symbolized by the raven.

Scáthach: (Celtic, "She Who Strikes Fear", "Shadowy One") Goddess of war and instructor/patroness of martial arts. Not much is written about Scáthach, except that she is native to the Isle of Skye and taught martial arts to Cú Chulainn, a great mortal hero in Irish literature. She is often associated with magic.

Deity of Wisdom/Magic

Wisdom and magic have often been linked in mythology, perhaps because it is only through wisdom that we can master the art of magic. Deities associated with these attributes are often intimidating. They offer us a glimpse into the unknown and into the deepest reaches of our soul, but such knowledge rarely comes without a price.

Athena/Athene: (Greek) Warlike goddess of wisdom and protector of cities, Athena was also patroness to craftsmen and seeker of justice. She was said to have been born, completely armed, out of the head of Zeus. Athena's connection between war and wisdom is obscure. One of her epithets includes "rouser of battle." Although she was considered the goddess of booty, Athena also reined over the art of peace. Athena is always portrayed wearing a helmet and carrying a spear and *aegis*, a magic goatskin with which she could flap terror into opposing forces and courage into her own. She is often associated with the owl, which even today symbolizes wisdom. Romans knew her as Minerva, who was originally an Etruscan goddess named Menerva. Minerva was also considered a patroness of medicine and trade.

Hekate: (Greek, "She Who Works from Afar", spelled Hecate in Latin) – Typically seen today as goddess of magic, ghosts, and hidden secrets and associated with the dark half of the moon, Hekate is one of the more misunderstood of the ancient Greek deities. Her name may not have originated in Greece, but in Asia Minor. She plays little part in legend and is not mentioned at all in the *Iliad* or the *Odyssey*. Dwelling at crossroads, tombs and the sites of violent crimes, often accompanied with the souls of the dead, her approach was said to be announced by the howling of dogs or the trembling of the ground. She is also identified with Artemis as a goddess of hunting. Under the title of Antaia ("She Who Meets"), she appears to travelers at night in lonely places as a terrible apparition.

Despite her fear-inspiring descriptions, Hekate was connected with the guardianship of women and the young and as the bestower and withholder of victory, pleasure and wealth. She is the only titan permitted by Zeus to remain in power. Hekate is represented in early Greek art as a single figure carrying a burning torch and clad in a long robe. Later, as a triple goddess, she is seen with three bodies standing back to back, sometimes as Maiden-Mother-Crone, although it is her Crone aspect that is most popular today.

Although her modern associations can be very different from what the early Greeks may have believed, this in no way lessens her modern incarnation. Even in ancient times, deities were known to change. The Egyptian god Thoth, for example, who was originally a moon god and measurer of time, later became a god of wisdom and knowledge.

Thoth: (Egyptian) God of writing, science, medicine, wisdom, and magic. Originally Thoth was a moon god and measurer of time, but gradually he was associated with wisdom and science. As secretary to the gods, Thoth recorded the judgement of the dead after their hearts were weighed against the Feather of Truth in the Hall of the Dead. The name Thoth is actually Greek – his Egyptian name is Tehuti or Djehuti.

Thoth is generally portrayed with the head of an ibis or as a baboon, often holding the reed pen and color palette of the Egyptian scribe. He is believed to have created alchemy and magic and assisted mortals by writing many books on astronomy, mathematics and medicine. The Greeks associated Thoth with the Greek god Hermes and as Hermes Trismegistas ("Thrice Great") – the source of the mystic revelations recorded in the hermetic literature of the Graeco-Roman period. These hermetic doctrines, said to contain the "ancient wisdom of Egypt", taught an understanding of god, man, and the universe, and how man, being a combination of god-like and mortal natures, was superior to the lesser gods.

Deity of Death/The Underworld

Often set apart from other deities, those associated primarily with death were both feared and worshiped. One of the earliest known depictions of death was found in a Neolithic settlement in Anatolia dating from the 7th millenium BCE, where death was represented as a flock of menacing giant black birds similar to vultures. Later deities of death were often closely associated with time since both time and death are inescapable. For example, in Iranian mythology, Zurvan, the god of time, is also the god of death. In Egypt, Thoth, who was originally associated with the passage of time, played an important part in the judgment of the souls of the recently deceased. Death is often associated with sleep, and in Greek and Roman mythology the gods of sleep and death were twin brothers.

Anubis: (Egyptian) God of the dead and of embalming, and protector of tombs, who leads the dead to the place of judgement where their hearts are weighed against the Feather of Truth. He is associated with divination and magic. Anubis is usually represented as a black jackal or dog, both of which roamed the cemeteries in the Egyptian desert. He is believed to be the inventor of embalming and the mummification process.

Charon: (Greek) The ferryman who carries the souls of the recently deceased across the river Acheron ("river of woe") into Hades, the underworld. It was customary to place an obolus (a silver coin) under the tongue or between the teeth of corpses to pay Charon's fare. Without it, the soul would be left to haunt the living, seeking release. Charon's appearance was close to demonic. According to the Roman poet Virgil, Charon, dressed in squalid garb, had a mass of unkempt, hoary hair on his chin and eyes that were staring orbs of flame. It is believed that Charon was originally a death god, as was his Etruscan counterpart, Charun, who appears on the walls of tombs holding a mallet with which he dealt the mighty death-blow to those destined to die. The memory of Charon lives on in modern Greek folklore as Charos, who carries off the young and old.

Donn: (Celtic, "The Brown, or Dark, One") God of death. Donn's home is on a small rocky island off the southwest coast of Ireland known as *Tech Duinn*, "The House of Donn", where he is isolated and aloof from the other gods. He is not a main character in early Celtic literature. Donn is a god of contrasting features being both benign, as protector of cattle and crops, and terrible, as creator of storms and shipwrecks. Revered as an ancestral deity of Ireland, Donn is identified with Daghdha ("Great Father"), from whom all Irish people descended. As a god of death, Donn was said to bind and carry off the dead. Caesar once associated Donn with Dis Pater, the Roman god of death.

Hades: (Greek, "The Unseen One") God of death and later the name of the underworld itself, which he ruled. Feared as merciless and unyielding, Hades had few followers and was rarely represented in art in fear of attracting his attention. However, he was not an unjust or destructive god despite his lack of pity. Although the *Iliad* mentions Hades as wandering the earth and living on Olympus, most Greek writers placed him almost constantly within the halls of the underworld. One of Hades' titles is *pluton*, which means "rich one" (or in Latin, *dis*, meaning "wealthy"). This is because the earth's wealth (precious metals and fertile crops) came from the ground; because of this, he was linked to the earth's fertility. Another common title for Hades was *orcus*, derived from the Greek word *horkos*, meaning "oath", because his name was used in oaths. The Romans equated Hades with Dis Pater.

Hel: (Norse): Goddess of death and ruler of Niflheim ("house of mists"), the place where the souls of those who did not die heroically went. (Those who died heroically went to Valhalla). Half her face is said to be that of a beautiful woman, but the other half that of a corpse. The entrance to Niflheim is guarded by a terrible dog named Garm. Although feared by the Vikings, she was worshiped by the common people, who held her as benevolent. The Christian "Hell" was derived from the goddess Hel's name. However, instead of being icy and cold like Niflheim, the Hell of the Christians was often associated with fire.

Odin: (Norse) As god of the dead, Odin conducts the souls of those who die in battle to Valhalla either in his own form or is represented by his messengers, the Valkyries. Odin was also the god of wisdom, magic, and war. On the battlefield, he may show himself as an old man in a cloak. Later, as Wodan (as he was known in Germany), he was identified as the leader of the wild hunt, whose wolfhounds could be heard baying as they passed through the sky on stormy nights.

Despite also being the god of inspiration and ecstasy who brought the world the gifts of poetry and learning, Odin was a wandering, restless god who was at times not very trustworthy. His followers, the "berserks", whose tradition dates back before the Vikings, were warriors infamous for wearing the skins of bears while raging furiously into battle. The word berserk actually means "dressed in bear skins" but has come to imply a type of blind fury. Both men and animals were sacrificed to Odin, who, according to legend, sacrificed himself to obtain knowledge for the gods and men, which included the runes. Odin had even sacrificed an eye in return for a drink from the well of wisdom.

Among his symbols were the horse and eagle (representing his power to travel between the worlds and over the sky), the spear, wolf and raven (which are linked with the battlefield), the three-way knot (indicating his magic power to bind), and a maiden with a horn or cup in her hand to welcome the dead (representing the joyous entry into Valhalla). He is also known as Othinn and Wotan.

Thanatos: (Greek) God of death. In Greek mythology, Thanatos is personified as death in two forms. Homer refers to the *ker thanatoio* ("fate of death") as a winged harpy that snatched away its victims in its huge claws. He was also portrayed less menacingly as a winged youth, clad in black robes, armed with a sword. Although he is the personification of death, Thanatos has a kind disposition towards mankind and is seen as bringing release from sickness and suffering.

The Roman equivalent of Thanatos is Mors. According to legend Mors shares residence in a remote cave beside the river Lethe with his twin bother Somnus, god of sleep. The traditional image of death personified as the Grim Reaper derives from Ovid's description of Mors as a hideous, cadaverous figure dressed in winding sheets (like the dead) and holding a scythe and hourglass.

Deity of Virility/Sexuality

Many of the gods associated with sexual potency were horned, or were symbolized by horned animals. Many horned animals will respond ferociously to danger, and males have a tendency to fight to the death – even when seriously injured – when attacked by another species. This savage behavior even in the face of certain death deeply impressed the ancient hunters, as did the sexual

exuberance of male horned animals. Horns were
considered symbols of physical power and sexual
force. Many early Celtic and Norse helmets were
adorned with horns in the belief that those
attributes would be instilled upon the warrior.
Horns were also associated with the erect phallus,
another symbol commonly associated with gods of
fertility.

Cernunnos: (Celtic, "Horned One") Although
associated with the Celts, the image of a horned
god dates back throughout history in Europe. He
is lord of all living creatures and is often portrayed
as an antlered figure sitting cross-legged and
surrounded by animals, including a snake with a
ram's head. Cernunnos is the god of nature,
virility and fertility and is associated with
shamanism and the underworld. Later he was
seen as the consort of the Great Goddess, and in
British folklore he was known as Herne. Merlin
has also been associated with this god due to his
affinity with nature and animals, especially the
stag.

Dionysius: (Greek) God of fertility, wine, and
ecstatic frenzy, Dionysius was known to the
Romans as Bacchus and is believed to be of
Thracian origin. He is the god of hidden desires
and passions and of the darker side of our
personality. Behind the wild rites of Dionysius
lies the recognition that we at some time or
another need to be released from the bonds of law
and order and social pressures and just let go.

Although usually thought of today as a jovial
drunk, Dionysius had a savage side to him that
was without mercy. Those that denied him risked
madness and he is said to have taken delight in
bloodshed. Although his worshipers could use

wine to find union with him, dance was the most potent and common means of union. Dionysius' cult, which penetrated Greece in Mycenean times, was known for their animal – and sometimes human – sacrifices where the carcass was torn to shreds and eaten. The cult, especially popular among women, performed wild dances at night on the top of mountains that lead to hysterical frenzies of ecstasy. Followers were often lawless and noisy, and thus tended to be unwelcome in towns. Later, Dionysius' wild nature was underplayed as he became, in Orphic philosophy, a god of immortality and rebirth.

Eros: (Greek) Often thought of as the god of love, Eros was in fact the god of passion, fertility, sexual potency, and desire. According to Greek mythology, Eros was one of the first gods to be brought into existence by Chaos, and had power even over the gods. Although not mentioned by Homer, the word *eros* was used in the *Iliad* and the *Odyssey* as meaning an irresistible physical desire. Eros was not only a creative agent, but also on occasions a very destructive one, reminding us of the power of passion to threaten order. Eros was often represented by his cult as a simple phallic figure. His symbol of the rose is quite revealing of his nature – being both delicate and fragrant, yet having sharp thorns.

To the Romans, Eros was seen as Cupid, who was less of a god and more of a mischievous child. Cupid could be vain and cruel, carrying two types of arrows: one golden and sharp that inspired love, and the other leaden and blunt, that produced fear and repulsion. He was known to use one of each on a couple so that the advances of one would repulse the other.

Min: (Egyptian) God of procreation and sexual potency – particularly male sexuality – as well as fertility of crops. Min is always portrayed with an erect phallus, sometimes with a flail raised in his right hand. The Egyptians closely associated the fertility of crops with human fecundity and so he was honored as lord of the harvest. Later Min was identified with roads and as the protector of travelers, often being identified with Horus. The Greeks equated Min with Pan.

Pan: (Greek, "Feeder of the Flocks") God of shepherds and hunters as well as fertility and human sexuality, Pan is portrayed as having a human body with the horns, ears, legs, and loins of a goat. He is the embodiment of pure instinct and tends to be lacking in his social graces. The lover of nymphs, Pan is said by Homer to have been dear to Dionysius, god of ecstasy and fertility. As a god of nature, Pan loved the mountains and other lonely places where he could practice his pipes, the syrinx, without disturbance. In his darker aspects he has been known to instill sudden terror on both men and animals, thus derived the word "panic." The Romans knew Pan as Faunus, who was one of Rome's most ancient nature gods. Faunus was also seen as the giver of oracles.

Deity as Destroyer/Chaos

Change is inevitable. Order is illusion. Paradoxically, those very things we fear most have been worshiped in the guise of certain deities. Perhaps it is through them that we can learn to except the fact that, for there to be creation, there must first be destruction.

Chaos: (Greek) The personification of the primordial void from which all things, including the gods, emerged. Although portrayed as male, Chaos is asexual, giving birth without the assistance of another. The concept of a primordial chaos can be found in a number of mythologies.

Kali: (Hindu) Also called Kali Ma, or Black Mother, Kali is the goddess of death and destruction – the manifestation of the Goddess in Her most terrifying and bloodthirsty aspect. Kali is a terrible but necessary destroyer as well as a powerful creative force. In her positive attributes, Kali is the destroyer of ignorance and a spiritual image for freedom and independence. To her worshipers, violence against women is strictly forbidden. Kali is the exterminator of demons and determines the destiny of all things. She represents the looming menace that lurks behind nature and is often portrayed as the mother who also punishes. She is also said to have invented the Sanskrit alphabet. Kali is usually portrayed with black skin, bare-breasted, and with four or more arms. Often she is portrayed carrying a sword in one hand and the severed head of Raktavija, the chief of the demon army, in another, while encouraging her worshipers, or carrying symbols of vitality, with her other hands. Sometimes she can be seen standing or dancing on the dead body of her husband, Shiva – even feasting on his intestines. Blood sacrifices, including human, have been made in her honor.

Nemesis: (Greek) Goddess of divine anger and daughter of Night (the goddess Nyx), Nemesis is the instrument through which the gods punished those who grew too proud through wealth and fame, or who angered the gods. Her vengeance is inflexible and inescapable. As time went on,

Nemesis gradually was softened into a kinder goddess of destiny, known as Adrasteia, "The Inevitable One", whom no one could escape. Adrasteia would bring sickness to those who abused their body and destruction to those parts of the earth we did not treat appropriately. Nemesis is also the goddess of law and retribution, often portrayed as a winged woman carrying a sword or whip and riding through the air on a chariot drawn by griffins.

Deity of Darkness or Related to Darkness

Not much is known about these deities, perhaps because the attributes that they personify are still a mystery to us today. Although they are the most unknown and mysterious of the deities, they are also the closest to us, lurking just behind the shadows of our unconscious.

Hypnos: (Greek) God of sleep, who brings us sleep by fanning his dark wings. He is son of Nyx, goddess of night, and is said to even have power over the gods, twice causing Zeus himself to sleep. Hypnos lives in the underworld with this twin brother Thanatos, god of death, and is portrayed either as a bearded man with wings attached to his shoulders or as a naked young man with wings attached to his temples. To the Romans, he was known as Somnus.

Moros: (Greek, "Destiny") Dark and unknowable god of destiny and personification of doom. He is all-powerful, and even the gods were susceptible to his power. Moros is brother to Thanatos, god of death, and son of Nyx, goddess of night.

Morpheus: (Greek, "He who forms") God of dreams, who can enter our minds while we are awake or sleeping and weave his spell to release us from the trappings of reality. Morpheus is responsible for shaping our dreams. To the ancient Greeks and Romans, dreams were regarded as one of the chief means whereby the gods could communicate with man. It was also a means by which man could foresee the future. Morpheus was the son of Hypnos, god of sleep, and grandson to Nyx, goddess of night. He was said to lie upon an ebony bed, surrounded by poppies, in a dimly lit cave.

Nyx: (Greek) Goddess and personification of night and darkness and daughter of Chaos. According to Greek mythology it was from Nyx that came the primeval silver egg which split in two to become the earth and sky. With Erebus, the personification of primeval darkness, she is mother to an assortment of abstract forces, such as death (Thanatos), sleep (Hypnos), destiny (Moros and Nemesis), deceit (Apate), and the Keres, avenging black winged female spirits of death and doom. Her realm lies in the furthest reaches of the west in the direction of the setting sun.

Deity as Trickster/Malicious Deities

I was originally going to exclude malicious deities, as well as the tricksters, since, due to their unstable nature, they are not usually worked with in magic. However, doing so would be hypocritical of Dark Paganism. Although these deities are usually not evoked, and when they are their attributes are often "softened" even by Dark Pagans, these deities play an important role. They represent the aspects of nature that we tend to avoid – the harshness of death, the instability of nature, and the fragility of life and the human condition. They are closest in form to true chaos. The mere fact that they are held as deities shows that the ancients, at least subconsciously, sensed this.

Ares: (Greek): God of war and violence, Ares was fond of strife and bloodshed. The ancient Greeks were not fond of this spiteful god who they referred to with such titles as "the shield-piercer" and "sacker of towns." Ares did not care who won the battle as long as blood was shed. Even Zeus, in the Iliad, tells Ares that of all the gods on Olympus, he found Ares the most distasteful. Ares is portrayed as a tall, handsome, yet vain, man. His chariot is pulled by Phobos (fear) and Deinos (terror).

While Athena stands for victory in battle through glory and honor, Ares epitomizes the evil and more brutal aspects of warfare.

Although the Romans identified Ares with the god Mars, there are several differences. Mars was originally a god of agriculture and continued to be seen as a protector of crops and cattle. Mars was also closely linked with the foundation of Rome itself; fathering the legendary founders of Rome (Romulus and Remus). Thus the Romans were known to consider themselves the "sons of Mars."

Eris: (Greek) Goddess of strife and discord, who took great pleasure in her work. Feared by most Olympians, Eris is believed to be the cause of the Trojan War. According to myth, Zeus refused to invite Eris to the wedding of Peleus & Thetis[1] due to her mischievous nature. In an act of retaliation, Eris threw a golden apple into the middle of the party as a prize to the most beautiful of the guests, many of whom were deities. When the goddesses Hera, Athena, and Aphrodite all vied for the prize, Zeus chose an anonymous shepherd from Troy named Paris as arbitrator. While Paris reflected, the goddesses each offered him bribes in order to win his favor. Athena offered him great power in battle, while Hera offered him great wealth. But Aphrodite offered Paris the hand of Helen, whose beauty was famous worldwide, and thus won the golden apple. Unfortunately Helen was already married to Menelaus, king of Sparta, and so Paris resorted to stealing his prize, which lead to retaliation and eventually the Trojan War.

Eris was Ares' constant companion, riding into battle with him. However, she is more often associated with less deadly forms of conflict such as rivalry and political unrest. The Romans knew Eris as Discordia, the personification of discord and strife. Today, Eris has found a following – or at least a certain amount of reverence – among Discordians, a group of Pagans that, to oversimplify, think we take life much too seriously. However, the Eris of Discordianism is viewed as far less baneful than the Eris of ancient Greece.

Lilith: (Hebrew, "She of the Night") Queen of demons and personification of feminine lust, Lilith

---

[1] Thetis was romantically involved with Zeus, but when Zeus was told that Thetis' son would become more powerful than his father, he married her off to Peleus, a grandson of Zeus.

was said to prey on newborn children who she would steal and kill. In essence, Lilith was the "bogeyman" to the children of ancient time. She was also linked to the succubae and vampires since she was believed to attack men who slept alone, seducing them and sucking their blood.

According to legend, before the creation of Eve, Adam had a wife named Lilith, who was created by God out of earth[1] like Adam. Lilith considered herself equal to Adam and refused to take the subordinate position of lying beneath him when they coupled, and finally flew away when he insisted. When Adam complained to God, three angels were sent to find Lilith and bring her back. Upon finding her beside the Red Sea, she was in the act of coupling with demons, giving birth to over one hundred demonic children a day. Lilith refused to return with the angels but promised not to harm newborn children that were near the inscriptions of the angels' names (Sanvi, Sansanvi, and Samangelaf). It was only then that God created Eve for Adam.

Despite her rather negative image, Lilith is now seen as an empowering source for feminine sexual liberation. It is only in modern times that Lilith was raised to the status of goddess. She was originally a demoness, and her presence was feared by young and old alike. While she retains much of her harsh approach and attitude, she is no longer considered evil, but rather free of social conditioning. Lilith is raw sexual energy that

---

[1] It is interesting to point out that ancient scholars often said Adam was made of earth but that Lilith was made of "filth and mud", no doubt to somehow justify their bias that Lilith, being woman, could not equal in status to Adam, who was a man.

reaches far beyond the role of procreation into the depths of desire and pleasure. She finds no shame in lust and sex for the pure sake of pleasure, but embraces it, personifies it.

While Lilith's modern associations may not warrant her to be placed under "Malicious Deities", it has been done not in disrespect, but simply since her nature is much harsher than a deity associated with fertility and sexuality.

Loki: (Norse) The trickster god. Loki was sly, deceitful, and extremely cunning, relying on his charm and wit to escape retribution for the trouble he frequently caused among the gods. He was not one to be trusted and was always extremely unpredictable and Machiavellian in his ways. Although not a magician, Loki was able to change into a variety of shapes including horse, falcon, and fly. He was completely amoral with no sense of honor, and is portrayed as a short handsome man with a friendly appearance. His titles included "The Trickster", "The Sly One", and "The Sky Traveler." After causing the death of the hero Balder, Loki was bound until his ultimate release at the end of the world (called Ragnarock), where he will play his role leading to the death of the gods.

Seth/Set: (Egyptian) Violent god of destruction, storms and drought, Seth was the personification of the dangers of the desert. Later he was regarded as the personification of evil, although never actually portrayed as a god of death. Seth was often depicted as an animal with pointed ears or horns and a long menacing muzzle and forked tail, and in later periods, he was identified with the dragon. Some believed he was protector of the caravans traveling through the desert, but he was also held responsible for sandstorms.

Part 2

Magic

The Nature of Magic

Magic is a very touchy subject since there are many ways to define and approach it. Through the evolution of the human mind, we have come to learn of ways to subtly influence our environment with various techniques we collectively call "magic." Various schools of thought, from folk magic to the Golden Dawn, have attempted to define the underlying principles and forces at play. Still, we are no closer to defining and documenting the underlying laws of nature on which it works.

Most magical practitioners would agree that the "supernatural" is not so much above the natural laws of the universe, but is merely above those laws and principles of nature that we currently comprehend. The term supernatural is but a metaphor to indicate our incomplete view of the "big picture."

No doubt our concept of the universe itself will need to change for us to grasp the true mechanisms of magic. Already such scientific revolutions as quantum mechanics have opened our minds to the possibility that the universe is not as clearly defined and neatly categorized as Newtonian physics has led us to believe. In fact, more and more the rift between science, metaphysics, and spirituality seems to be closing. Perhaps when this gap is closed we will finally realize the forces at work behind magic and better harness them.

Until then, those who practice magic are pioneers into this unknown realm. Through trial and error we have experimented as arcane scientists in hopes of perfecting our method. We have come to find some means that are effective, and even some theories that seem to make sense, but in the end we remain in the dark as to the universal truths that await us. Anyone who has seriously practiced magic has no doubt sensed the change in energy around them when working with these forces, although such energy cannot yet be detected with instruments.

The secret to working magic lies not in ancient grimoires or clandestine organizations, but in understanding and working with the nature of magic.

Law of Action

In order to successfully perform magic it is important that there be a specific need and intent. Without these there is no way for the practitioner to connect to the energies that will be raised. Simply put, it is the practitioner's intent and need for the magic that focuses and directs it. This is where the concept of magic can get complicated.

If, for example, you want to perform magic to accomplish something that can more easily be done without magic, the simple fact that this alternative was not taken would indicate that the practitioner does not have the intent necessary to perform the magic.

In other words, trying to turn off a light using magic when the switch is within walking distance guarantees failure. If you are not willing to reach for that switch, how can you have the intent necessary to work magic? The fact is, you don't – to do so would indicate the interest is not in the objective, but in the desire to play with magic simply to see results. Magic helps those who help themselves. This is what I like to call the *Law of Action*.

A true practitioner has the self-discipline to know when there is a need to use magic and when there is not. Magical practitioners are more concerned with the objective than the means and are willing to work towards that objective using any means possible, including taking physical action. If you are not willing to work towards your goal, how can magic possibly help you?

Magic also requires work even after the spell is cast – it is not an easy way out as some like to think. Casting a spell to break a bad habit is not enough to conquer it; it empowers the individual to better handle the situation, but that person still must make the effort necessary to finally conquer the bad habit.

The practitioner must be willing to make every effort to obtain these goals for him- or herself or the magic will lack potency. One must be willing to take advantage of opportunities that arise, and often take risks. Magic is far from being the "easy road" to success that many published spell books declare in order to sell. On the contrary, the experienced practitioner discovers that as one empowers oneself to reach one's goals, the need to perform specific acts of magic decreases. This is because such people have reached a point where their mere intention to accomplish a task is all they need to follow through. Magic then becomes a tool used for special needs such as healing, since such things rely on more than just physical action and confidence to achieve results.

Limitations of Magic

Any serious student of magic will have long since put behind ideas of shooting lighting bolts and mystically teleporting to various locations in the blink of an eye. As physical beings we are governed by certain natural laws, and although we must admit that science has not yet discovered all of these laws, we are nonetheless restricted to a physical plane. What this means is that even magic is limited in how it can affect the physical world. Keep in mind that these natural laws encompass more than we currently understand and includes what is called the "supernatural" – that which falls outside of our understanding.

Since the physical plane is governed by certain laws, for magic to affect the physical plane it must adhere to these laws. In doing so it will tend to take the simplest path. This does not rule out the possibility of a "miraculous event," but it does mean that such drastic results are far from common; nature in general has a tendency to take the path of least resistance.

Keeping the example of the light switch from the previous section, if for some reason a spell was successfully cast to turn off a light, the result would manifest most likely by someone noticing the light was on and turning it off; it is very unlikely that the switch would just move of its own accord. Magic works very subtly and although we can attempt to control the end result, we cannot control the way the result will manifest. Perhaps the light will burn out or there will be a blackout or blown fuse. Perhaps you forgot to pay the electric bill and it just so happed the electric company decided now was the time to turn off actual services. The possibilities are endless, but the manifestations will typically be simple and often seem the product of a well-timed coincidence.

Until the limitations of magic are accepted the practitioner will continue to be disappointed with the results of magic work. True magic bares little resemblance to what is portrayed in Hollywood, yet it can still be a powerful tool for change. Hence, when working magic it is recommended one concentrate on the *objective* and not the means to that objective. Attempting to control the exact outcome of a spell will result in failure since nature itself will not tolerate restrictions.

Psychological Factors of Magic

Magic works on many levels, and a wise practitioner will take advantage of them all. Many refuse to accept the psychological aspects of magic in fear that it in some way invalidates magic from being real.

In truth, a large portion of the effects of magic is psychological in origin. Spells for self-improvement, such as breaking a bad habit or finding a job for example, are motivational as well as magical. Don't underestimate the power of positive thinking. The very construct of a spell or ritual specifically and intentionally plays on both a psychological as well as metaphysical level.

By working magic one is able to visualize the objective and declare one's intent to reach that goal. By performing the magic we hardwire this intention into our psyche using symbolism we find empowering. Between the energy being raised and the sense of confidence provided by the belief that the magic will help, we find ourselves more enabled in reaching that goal. It boosts our self-confidence and overcomes many of our own self-created obstacles, such as fear and doubt. As the saying goes, we are our own worst enemy. We build psychological walls to protect ourselves and thus restrict our potential. When we are forced to overcome such barriers we find ourselves amazed at what we can achieve. Often it takes great hardship for us to break free of our self-imposed limitations, for there is no greater motivational tool than the fight for survival.

The study of magic seeks to break these same barriers within us. We seek to understand who we are as a whole and accept even those harsh and unwanted areas of our personality. Only then can we truly define what it is we desire or need. Only then can we honestly seek to reach our goals and unlock our potential to do so.

Another psychological aspect of magic often ignored is the use of imagery or tools that promote a sense of empowerment. This symbolism triggers a psychic response much like certain smells or memories can trigger intense nostalgia. The smell of incense, the lighting of a candle, the ringing of a ritual bell – these can all trigger a response in our psyche that quickly brings us to a mental state suitable for magic. When these triggers are not present, visualization can often provide an effective substitute.

So, too, are there personal cues that affect us in a similar way. Perhaps we get goosebumps when using a sword to direct energy rather than an athame, perhaps a certain garment or jewelry makes us feel magical, or certain visualizations empowering. These effects are triggered by unconscious associations. Sometimes they may make sense, other times they do not. Someone who is aware of how certain senses affect him or her can make use of them to trigger a change of consciousness or to raise more energy during magic.

To wear black in ritual because is looks nice or because it is "traditional" is quaint; to wear black because doing so makes one feel more in tune to the mysteries of the universe is profound. Every tool, every movement, every uttered phrase should have personal meaning to the practitioner. Reciting a spell should elicit goosebumps as the words ring deep into our unconscious awakening our souls as they tap into the archetypal energies that lurk there. We can't do this consciously – we simply must discover them through trial and error, hence the importance of a journal where we can outline our workings and reflect on our responses. Anything that elicits a sense of awe, wonder, or power should not be taken for granted. Such things are they key to connecting to the magic work.

Magic is, after all, both a science and an art. It is a science because it relies on certain principles and theories learned though observation and trial and error. It is an art in that in order to be effective one must develop one's own style and form using the aforementioned principles and theories in a manner that is most effective for the individual.

Emanations

Until now I have not mentioned concepts such as telepathy and empathy since they have become trendy keywords in new age practice and are rarely explored in a substantial matter. This chapter, which is geared for metaphysical exploration, provides an opportunity to explore these phenomena in a new light.

The aura, empathy, telepathy – these all rely on the same principle: emanation. We are surrounded by a cloud of "psychic noise" and stray energies that emanates from our being. This culmination is commonly refereed to as "the aura" in an attempt to oversimplify this phenomenon. This aura consists of many layers and derives from many sources. Some of these emanations have been scientifically documented while others are debated or denied.

The most well known and easily sensed of these emanations is heat. On the physical plane, life is essentially a mechanical process. Our bodies burn fuel derived from food producing heat. The body maintains a certain threshold temperature at its core in order to sustain the various life functions within, therefore we radiate heat energy at different levels throughout our body.

Included in these natural life processes is the generation and flow of electrical currents via our nervous system. Although more subtle and thus harder to detect, we emanate a certain amount of electromagnetic energy. This too can be detected and explained scientifically. In fact, some animals can sense the electromagnetic energy of living creatures to hunt for food.

There are, however, other forms of energy that have not yet been detected externally, but have been accepted within occult and metaphysical sciences as real and substantial. These include thought and emotion. Within the scientific community both thought and emotion are detected in how they affect the physical body and our perception. The electrical signals produced in the brain by thoughts can be detected, but the nature and content of those thoughts can not. However, one may be able to insinuate the type of thoughts by their physical manifestation such as body language and tone of voice. (The clenching of a fist, for example, could indicate anger.) Likewise, emotions trigger the release of hormones and other chemicals into the body that cause a change in its operation (flushing of skin, perspiration, change in breathing and heart rate). Again, these are only physical manifestations of something more encompassing.

The detection of these more subtle energies is labeled telepathy for the reception of external thoughts, and empathy for the reception of external emotions. Both terms have been warped and exaggerated by those wishing to obtain these abilities. Ironically, we all possess the innate ability to detect external thoughts and emotions, albeit on a very subtle level which varies with the individual. The point is not so much to increase our natural ability but to learn how to quiet our mind and sense it apart from our own emanations. Since these emanations are subtle we are not always able to determine the exact thought or emotion, but rather sense that someone is lying or upset. Our "gut feeling" may, for example, warn us of malicious intentions behind a seemingly amicable exterior. ("There is something about that person...")

Intuition is the unconscious conclusions drawn from the obvious physical signs as well as the emanations of others. Our unconscious mind often combines the various senses of these emanations along with our memory and physical senses to reach a more specific conclusion than casual observation itself could ascertain. We may unconsciously register subtle body language or changes in tone of voice that are only realized later upon reflection. This should not be discounted. Such a sense, be it "psychic" or not, can be of great use, particularly since we are not always able to distinguish external thoughts and emotions from our own. Thus it is typically easier for us to learn to trust this overall feeling than to try to control the internal processes from which the sense derived.

The "aura" itself is a combination of all these emanations which includes heat, electromagnetism, thought, emotion, and will, among others. Color is often used metaphorically and visually to better label and determine what we sense unconsciously. The color itself is not actually present as many who "see" auras have claimed. Since many tend to work well in using visualization to see this field of energy, many unconsciously use the technique and so may confuse visualization with actual sight. The actual colors are relative to our own personal associations to those colors. For example, one is not glowing red when they are angry, but someone who associates red with anger may sense a red aura in such a case: there is no invisible red light actually around the observed person.

Some people work well with such visualizations and can thus visualize such perceptions automatically. Others choose not to even make such associations with color but to simply experience the sense as one's own, such as with natural empaths.

Some people are naturally empathic or telepathic and do not realize it. Naturally empathic individuals, for example, may suddenly feel nervous when interviewing someone for a position, or pass a group of teens waiting for a school bus and suddenly feel insecure or watched without reason (a feeling common during puberty), or find themselves getting more and more angry in an argument as the anger/frustration of the other person feeds our own.

Such people must learn how to differentiate their own feelings from those emanating from others around them. They may take emotionally charged situations personally and often have a tendency to avoid crowded areas or areas/situations that elicit negative emotions or stress, such as rush hour traffic and holiday shopping.

Often awareness of empathic or telepathic abilities itself lessens the effectiveness of those same abilities. When we consciously attempt to sense an external thought or emotion we become distracted by our own thoughts, feelings, doubts, and biases. It is best to keep such processes unconscious and learn to react according to our intuition or "gut feeling". Our unconscious mind is constantly throwing out thoughts and ideas – some are mere fantasy and wishful thinking, others may stem from our shadow or various slight neuroses we all harbor in one form or another (bad habits, paranoia, pet peeves). These glimpses of insight are often drowned out by the other voices (including ego, the shadow, and various complexes). Throughout the process of discovering ourselves we can learn to silence the day-to-day chatter in our minds to better hear and distinguish our intuition and insight. We also learn to trust ourselves and act according to our instinct and nature. When we try to listen actively to these voices we spend too much time listening to and processing every thought, which proves distracting if not overwhelming. To complicate matters, sometimes thoughts/feelings that seem foreign to us are still our own; aspects of ourselves like the shadow are not conscious to us and yet influence our mind with their own voices.

We all have experienced times when we have gone against our gut feeling only to later say "I knew I should have done..." Hindsight is always more clear than foresight.

Essence of Being

Although we exist on a physical plane, we are not solely physical objects; there is more to us than the mere physical. For example, we have thought and emotions that lie beyond physical explanation. In essence, we are composed of three aspects: Physical, Intellectual, and Spiritual.

These aspects are not just conceptual structures – they are metaphors for the types of energies from which all things are composed. They are also levels of consciousness connecting to (or communing with) these energies. One may even argue that on a grander scale they are dimensions unto themselves – levels of existence where concepts of such things as astral planes and the afterlife take root.

We cannot define ourselves by these individual aspects but only by the interaction of all three. The Self transcends each level becoming something more than the sum of its parts. If the aspects of being were seen as waves of energy, the Self would be the "interference" when these three waves collided. In this sense, Self is not static but constantly in flux. For this reason many religions and spiritual teachings believe the Self to be an illusion: it is not a clearly definable "thing" but the result of the interaction of the various aspects of our Being. Each aspect itself is also not clearly defined; our perception and sense of identity are all that maintain this semblance of static reality.

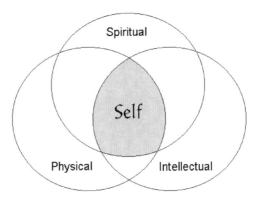

Figure 5: Essence of Being

Our physical essence is rather simple – what you see is what you get. It consists of our physical body and the mechanics of the brain and internal organs. As our link to the physical world, it is how we interact with the environment and is the basis of our perceptions of the (physical) universe. Our physical aspect is what exists entirely in space and time and thus is governed by the laws of the physical universe, both the laws that are known and those yet to be discovered by science. Without the other aspects, the physical aspect is nothing more than a lifeless puppet, because it must be acted upon to function.

Our intellectual (or mental) essence is manifested in our thoughts and intellect. It includes our reasoning abilities and awareness. The intellectual aspect is what binds our physical aspect to the spiritual, as a sort of intermediary. Much of our personality and the ego are developed here, although they are rooted in the spiritual. The concept of "mind" could be considered the interaction of our intellectual and spiritual aspects, while base instincts and passions are predominantly the interaction between the physical and the intellectual.

Unlike our physical aspect, our intellectual aspect has no limits except those that it chooses to create, for it defines its own limits and reality. Since our intellectual aspect can see in an unlimited number of perspectives, our potential for knowledge or ideas has no boundaries. The intellectual aspect is consciousness itself and the birthing place of self-awareness. It is through our intellectual aspect that we are able to interact with the physical world through our physical aspect. The intellectual aspect is what gives us a sense of identity.

Although our ego and consciousness give our intellectual aspect a certain amount of momentum of its own, the intellectual aspect exists primarily as a function of the spiritual level, which requires an intermediary to link to the physical.

Our spiritual essence is harder to define because, of the three, it is the "furthest" from the physical world with which we are familiar. Some like to refer to our spiritual aspect as the "Divine Spark" since it is the life force – that which is behind life itself. It IS life – without it the mechanics of the body loses its momentum, becoming an empty shell. It is the spark that ignited the big bang – when nothingness became something. It is what sets things in motion – from the universe to the smallest particles that make up the atoms. It is the great unknowable force, the structure within chaos, that shaped the various chemical compounds of the primordial seas into the first life forms and then instigated the evolution of the countless forms of life we now have. It is the pure energy from where the other aspects of being derive – the true source of creation and existence. Through the symbolism of many religions, we have come to best grasp this Great Unknowable through such concepts as Brahman, the Tao, YHWH ("I am who am"), or the Creatrix. The more we attempt to define it the less we grasp its true nature.

The spiritual aspect is not a part of space and time and so is the source of psychic awareness and intuition. It is the part of us that connects us to creation and thus to each other. However, since in our daily life the perspective of our intellectual aspect is predisposed towards the physical, we are naturally biased towards that plane. Thus we cannot fully comprehend the spiritual aspect, although during meditation, or moments of natural self-reflection, the perspective of the intellectual aspect is redirected inward towards the spiritual aspect. A spiritual experience could be considered a dramatic but temporary shift of perspective towards our spiritual aspect. Where the intellectual aspect gives us individuality, the spiritual aspect is what connects us to creation.

Within our spiritual aspect also lies the ability to work magic. The significance of the concept of the Essence of Being in magic will become apparent in the next chapter, *The Structure of Magic.*

At this point you may be wondering where emotions fit in. Emotions are not an aspect of Being: they are forms of energy that manifest at the core of what we call the "Self" and emanate both outward and into each aspect of Being. They are caused by the interaction of our Self with the various aspects of Being.

No one essence is more important than the other. It is the balancing interaction of all our aspects that gives us our sense of Self. While denying the physical has long been used to bring us closer to the spiritual, it can leave us out of balance: we lose touch with what we truly are as a whole. Of course, the opposite is also true; we cannot hope to get closer to the spiritual if we get caught up in the physical trappings.

Even the intellectual aspect has its extreme. Attempting to fully comprehend the spiritual only distances us from its true nature. Many kabbalists and ceremonial magicians become so caught up in concepts that they lose sight of their true objective.

Denying *any* part of our being to become closer to another leaves us out of balance and thus incomplete. As humans we are composed of all three and we must accept that in order to grow.

Although these aspects appear very different from one another, they are actually manifestations of the same creative energy, wherein the mystery of our Being lies. All things contain these essences to various degrees, although on the physical plane it is humans who significantly possess the intellectual aspect that allows them to transcend the physical to some extent. However, this trait comes not without a cost. It is because of our complex intellect that we can easily become out of balance. On a larger scale, we can see that humanity (outside of the dwindling tribal cultures) is already out of balance and has lost much of its connection to the earth, their bodies, and their spirituality.

We too are animals, separated only by our superior reasoning abilities that allow us self-reflection. It is through this self reflection that consciousness can exist on more than one plane, while the consciousness of other animals appears to exist solely on the physical plane. However, don't mistake this as being spiritually superior. Other animals, whose intellects do not go far beyond that of instinct[1], are in constant balance unless we interfere with their lives. They are completely at one with their natures. Humans, on the other hand, are closest to their true nature at birth and drift away from it as they develop due to various social conditionings. In order to return to our true nature we are forced to unlearn much of what we have learned, leading to the need for dark paths.

As a species we seem to have lost our collective nature. Our intellectual development surpassed our spiritual development throwing us out of balance. We are now reaching an important stage in our development as a whole. We have begun to grasp our insignificance in the cosmos but also the significance of our actions on earth. Slowly we are accepting the responsibility we have to maintain the fragile balance of our ecosystem. For too long our species has existed as a virus on this planet. Perhaps such deadly diseases as cancer and AIDS are the planet's "immune system"

---

[1] One may argue that some animals, such as dolphins, are in fact highly intelligent. Regardless of this, the fact remains that the more advanced the intellectual aspect, the greater the potential of losing balance since only the intellectual aspect can act against its nature through such things as the imposition of self-created limits.

fighting back. Unless we as a species attain balance, we will either be forced to infect other worlds or face extinction in our own waste.

As individuals, few of us will realistically make a difference, but perhaps as more and more of us break free from out-dated social conditioning to find our own paths, we will challenge the collective to reflect upon itself and its ideals. The one saving grace we have – self-reflection – has the ability to return us to our center. Already the seeds have been planted. The American culture's growing obsession with gothic imagery signifies our unconscious desire to find the truths that lurk in the darkness of our minds. Perhaps the adolescent species called "man" will seek the path to maturity and not self-destruction. The true age of enlightenment is almost upon us and we, the children of the night, are its pioneers.

The Structure of Magic

There are probably more definitions of magic than there are magical systems. For simplicity, magic is the use of will to achieve change. This, of course, leaves much room for interpretation, as is intended.

Although there are numerous magical systems, it doesn't take long to see that there are certain basic underlying principles common to all. Many established systems have perfected their techniques through trial and error and are worth study. Some systems are so tightly interwoven with religious or cultural beliefs that it is difficult to separate the techniques from, or comprehend them without, these beliefs. This is another reason why the New Age movement can be dangerous: although it opens the door to learning new practices from all over the world, it often attempts to strip or water down the cultural aspects of the various spiritual and magical practices. As a specific form of spiritual practice becomes popular, such as with shamanism, it becomes a fad and is altered even more in order to better sell related books and merchandise.

The actual structure to performing magic is quite simple; the difficulty lies in finding the right technique for the individual. This is no easy matter and it would be wise to keep some sort of journal.

There are four basic steps in performing magic:

1. Establish a Receptive State of Consciousness ("Proper Frame of Mind")

2. Raise Energy

3. Direct Energy

4. Ground and Center

These steps may be combined depending on the technique being used, but the concept remains the same.

As discussed in the section *"Essence of Being"* of the previous chapter, we are composed of three aspects: Physical, Intellectual, and Spiritual, where each aspect is a different manifestation of the same creative energies.

Magic relies on a cycle of transcending to the spiritual and returning to the physical. The following chart shows the interplay of the aspects of Being with the four stages of magic.

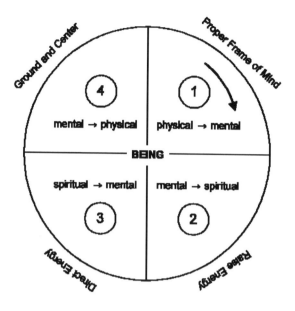

Figure 6: Correlation of the Flow of Consciousness and Essence of Being with Stages of Magic.

Each stage in the working of magic creates a bridge between connecting aspects of our Being. Upon successfully working magic, we have transcended to the spiritual, where lies the source of all magic, and returned to the physical where the magic will eventually manifest.

In the first stage we are relaxing the body and moving into deeper levels of consciousness where we can begin to tap into our spiritual essence. Once we have altered our consciousness to a state that is more receptive, we can connect with the spiritual to draw power in the second stage. In order to apply this energy we must, in the third stage, direct this energy back toward the physical, using the intellect as the bridge. Finally, in the fourth stage, we return to the physical plane, where we can continue to work towards our goal.

This flow of consciousness is also evident in the casting of a circle. As the circle is cast, we traverse the cycle of consciousness in the essence of Being – it is a microcosm of the same flow of energy in the process of magic itself. Life, magic and the spiritual journey all flow in cycles consisting of cycles within cycles and thus we have the spiral dance.

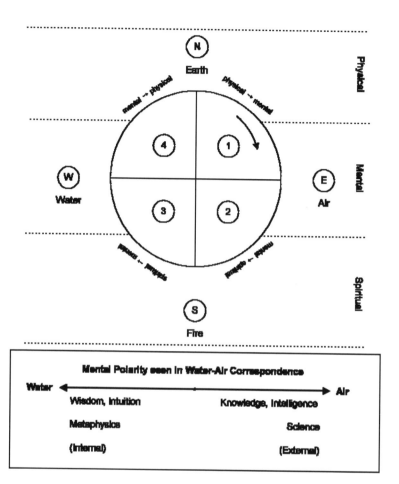

Figure 7: Correlation of the Flow of Consciousness in Magic to the Elements/Quarters of the Circle

Note that both Water and Air are associated with the Intellectual (or Mental[1]) aspect of Being. Keep in mind that emotions, which are traditionally associated with Water, are not one of the essences

---

[1] I use "mental" and "intellectual" synonymously when discussing this aspect of our Being. Neither word fully fits, but these two seem most adequate since this is the aspect that encompasses the mind beyond the physical mechanics of the brain.

of Being, but rather a byproduct of the interactions of these aspects or energies. Air reflects the perspective of the intellectual aspect from the physical while Water reflects the physical aspect from the spiritual.

STEP 1: ESTABLISHING A RECEPTIVE STATE OF CONSCIOUSNESS

Before beginning any sort of magic work, it is a good idea to be in the right frame of mind. Wiccans like to refer to this mindset as being "between the worlds." At this point, the practitioner has shed the mundane trappings and is more in touch with the silence that is in the center of our Being. It is a trance-like state similar to meditation but allows one to remain active. Once in this altered state of consciousness, the practitioner is better prepared to begin the process of raising the actual energy.

There are many ways to achieve this receptive state, and often they are used in combination. These techniques can be broken down into the following categories:

- Meditation/Visualization

- Ritualized Movement

- Music/Sound

- Physical Cues

- Mind-altering Substances

Meditation/Visualization

Meditation makes use of various relaxation techniques in order to expand the consciousness. Proper meditation clears the mind, allowing one to shed the mundane thoughts that crowd it. Whereas many of the below techniques also relax and clear the mind, meditation takes us one step further by getting us in touch with that inner silence. The below techniques are often used to prepare the mind for meditation, as well as magic working.

Repetition - The repetition of sounds, such as the classic "aum" (or "om") or chants, lulls the mind into a more receptive state. The underlying meaning of the sound or chant can then help guide the mind into a mindset more in tune with that meaning. Therefore chanting about the moon, for example, would be an excellent means of preparation before working magic involving the moon. Repetitive movements can also be used.

Concentration - Like many relaxation techniques, concentrating on a mental image or physical object (such as a flame or bowel of water) for an extended period of time allows the brain to wander from its usual thought patterns, providing the individual some freedom from the usual thought traffic. In other words, it "bores" the mind, and does not allow it to find other thoughts to keep it occupied. Eventually the mind "gives in" and one's consciousness sinks inward. This technique is often used in scrying, which in itself is a form of meditation.

Breathing - Breathing is used in any relaxation technique to relax the body and thus eventually relax the mind, especially when one's concentration is focused on the breath. Usually, controlled breathing consists of inhaling through the nose, expanding the diaphragm (not the chest) to draw in the air, and then exhaling through the mouth. It is best to let the body regulate the actual pace of the breathing. It will naturally begin to slow and deepen as the body relaxes. Many have found touching the tip of the tongue to the roof of the mouth during inhalation to be helpful when working with energy. This is a popular practice in Eastern beliefs when working with *ch'i,* or life energy.

Visualization - Visualization allows us to take ourselves, at least from the mind's perspective, somewhere that is more conducive to magic work, such as a temple, forest, or alchemical laboratory – whatever images remind us of magic. Not only can we use visualization to guide our meditation, but we can draw upon these images to help alter consciousness. For example, just as imagining being on a beach watching a sunset can actually be physically relaxing, so too will some people feel empowered and more receptive to working magic when imagining oneself in a certain place. These images, of course, are a personal matter. If you find yourself daydreaming of certain places, they may be of use in such visualizations.

Visualization can also be used in conjunction with breathing. Many forms of meditation visualize the inhalation of light (usually white or blue), symbolizing positive or healing energy, and the exhalation of negative energy (usually using a color or shade the individual associates with negativity). This same use of color in visualization can be used to surround the body or slowly work its way up the body as a relaxation technique. As the light envelopes a body part, that part of the body becomes relaxed.

Ritualized Movement

When every action and word is deliberate and has meaning, the mind begins to alter consciousness to one more receptive to spiritual or magic work. Ritualized movement can be as simple as the smudging of an individual or the performing of an elaborate ritual.

The physical act of casting a circle not only marks the workspace, but helps to prepare the mind for magic work. Often, even the way one moves within the circle is ritually significant. For example, many will only walk in a deosil, or sun-wise, direction while in the circle.

Ritually bathing, which is often used as a ritual means of cleansing negativity, also helps to alter consciousness, especially when done in candlelight, perhaps using scented oils or incense. The warmth and soothing sound of the water relaxes the body and mind, making it more receptive to change. Water is a universal symbol for cleaning and purification as well as life.

Martial arts, when practiced correctly, have an internal, and in some ways spiritual aspect. The katas of Karate or the forms of T'ai Chi Ch'uan are very useful as active meditations. They relax the mind and promote the flow of life energy.

Dancing to tribal drums has been used throughout history by many cultures to induce a trance-like state seen in ecstatic dancing. The physical assertion, coupled with the rhythm of the drums, has a profound affect on the consciousness. It is possible to become so involved with the music that the dancing becomes spontaneous and unconscious. Anyone who has attended one of the many large Pagan gatherings cannot help but notice how involved many get around the fire drums. Dancing to other forms of music can be just as effective. The music, if any, should be something the practitioner finds personally empowering.

Processions, either in a group or alone, to the location of the workspace can help to induce an altered state of consciousness. Processions can be in silence or accompanied by chanting or singing. The focus should be in the attitude – you are not just walking, you are in a procession, and so an attitude of reverence or respect is necessary. (This reverence does not have to be for a deity, but can be for the power that is about to be tapped.) The pace should be somewhat slow and deliberate and in the case of a group, everyone should be walking at the same pace where possible. The distance itself does not need to be long, as long as enough time is given to induce the desired change in consciousness.

A nice addition that I have seen added to some Wiccan circles is for the procession to pass through a "gate" of people on either side. This gate blesses the people, usually with the elements (incense or smudge for fire/air and saltwater for earth/water), as they pass into the circle. This heightens the sensation of "crossing over" into a place between the worlds, particularly when each person is also anointed with oil when entering the circle.

7
Music/Sound

Music has the remarkable ability to affect us emotionally and physically. In movies, it enhances the story by directing our emotions in ways that bond us with the characters. In the same manner, some music can relax us or empower us. In preparing for magic, music can be a useful tool in setting the atmosphere to one conducive to the work about to be done. It can also be played in the background during the work itself to help maintain the desired atmosphere.

The actual choice of music will depend on the individual's tastes and reaction to the music. The importance is in the reaction, not the music itself.

Physical Cues

We often use physical cues without realizing it. Candles and incense, for example, have been used by almost every religion and magical system throughout history[1]. We often have a very Pavlovian reaction to them in that they tend to subtly influence our mind towards a more spiritual or magical leaning. Used in ritual they become fundamental tools towards the required change in consciousness.

Subdued lights, the smell of incense burning, the sight of an altar prepared for ritual – these act as

---

[1] Actually oil lamps were used more than candles in ancient times since they lacked the chemicals needed to help wax keep its shape and the costs were often too high. The dim flickering flame effect is the same, however.

cues to our unconscious, preparing the mind for the work to come. Through time the practitioner may learn of other more personal cues that are often more effective.

Mind-altering Substances

Probably the most controversial means of altering one's consciousness, the use of mind-altering substances, especially in shamanistic practices, is universal. This section would be sorely incomplete without at least a brief discussion on this topic.

Legalities aside, there is nothing intrinsically *wrong* with using mind-altering substances in magic work. In fact, used properly it can be quite effective. However, the proper use is what is at issue. Our culture is ill-equipped in the use of drugs for magic. Its potential for abuse and misuse is quite high. Unlike shamans, who have been raised in the teachings of its use, we have no such foundation. Without such a strong foundation in the use of these substances, the practitioner is left with blind experimentation.

Should this avenue be explored, the practitioner can expect to encounter certain obstacles that will need to be addressed. These issues should be dealt with long before the use of any mind-altering substance.

Unlike other means of altering consciousness, the use of mind-altering substances cannot be controlled in the same manner. Its effects are far from subtle and very unstable. In order to take advantage of this state of mind, the practitioner must be extremely strong of will and self-control.

In addition, the practitioner will constantly need to be aware of what is real and what is hallucination. No mater how powerful the magic, one simply cannot fly. As humorous as this may sound, while under the influence of a mind-altering substance, the distinction between reality and fantasy is far from clear: what may be thought to be a spiritual experience could be nothing more than a drug-induced hallucination.

Needless to say, the practitioner should not be working magic while experimenting with the drug for the first time. It is also not a good idea to be experimenting with *any* substance without someone present who is not using any mind-altering substances. Safety is of utmost importance and all experimentation should be planned well beforehand. The observer should be clear on when it would be appropriate to intervene and what actions should be taken. Should the practitioner insist on working alone, it is *highly* recommended that a note be carried that indicates what substance and dosage was taken, and at what time, in the event of an unforeseen complication – medical or otherwise. The magic work itself should be kept simple to avoid risk of injury. Candles – or any source of fire – should only be used if an observer is present.

Before experimenting with mind-altering substances, the practitioner should research the effects and dosages as well as determine a safe way of obtaining them. Since these sources will tend to be questionable, the authenticity of the substance is also an issue.

Mescaline, although long lasting (6-8 hours), is rather safe and not physically addictive. (Anything can be psychologically addictive – people with addictive personalities should avoid drugs.) "Ecstasy", a more modern synthetic drug, is similar to mescaline but its effects are much shorter lasting depending on the dosage and "brand". Both are hallucinogens. Natural substances such as peyote and mushrooms should be avoided unless being instructed by someone *personally* familiar with their use – books tend to not be a reliable substitute.

The use of mind-altering substances is best left to the more seasoned student. Beginners must focus their energy on mastering the various other techniques first. Relying on drugs to change one's consciousness merely indicates that the practitioner has not developed the skills necessary to perform magic effectively. In such a case, mind-altering substances may give the *illusion* of power, but there will be *no* magic. These substances have the potential of being useful in magic, but to the novice, it can be equated to a child playing with fire. The constant reliance on mind-altering substances makes for poor development of the disciplinary skills needed to work magic.

Apart from the use of hallucinogens or other mind-altering substances, alcohol – particularly wine – is a very common element in ritual. Usually this is limited to a few sips or a cup full and thus the effects, at most, is a slight relaxing of the mind. Since alcohol is a depressant, it is not recommended in larger quantities. Unlike hallucinogens, alcohol deadens the body and mind making the individual very ineffective in magic. Also, when working with a group, keep in mind that there is always the possibility of an alcoholic being present. To such people even a sip of wine can have devastating effects long after the ritual. To be safe, all present should be given the option of not drinking or better yet, use juice.

STEP 2: RAISING ENERGY

There are two basic approaches to the raising of energy: internal and external.

Internal raising of energy refers to the drawing of energy from within the practitioner. The practitioner is the one doing the empowering.

External raising of energy refers to the drawing of energy from outside the practitioner, such as from an object or from a deity, spirit, or archetype.

Technically, even the external raising of energy requires a certain amount of internal working as well, but it is more the approach that I am exploring here. *Any* magic working relies on the practitioner to some extent, who is charged with raising the energy and then later using it to achieve a goal.

Some magical systems, such as is used by many Wiccans, make use of both techniques depending on the situation. Usually spells are internally oriented and rituals, where the Goddess and God are invoked, are more external in design.

Often, the acts of raising energy go hand in hand with the first step – establishing the proper frame of mind. Circle casting not only helps define a space, and prepare the practitioner for the working, it also provides a framework in which to build and focus energy. Ecstatic dancing not only produces a trance-like state, but also serves as a powerful tool for building energy.

The power of the orgasm has, throughout history, been used for magical, as well as spiritual, purposes. This can be achieved alone, through masturbation, or with a partner or partners. Unfortunately, this technique is often abused. This topic is explored more fully in the chapter on *Basic Sex Magic*.

Incantations are a very simple and effective way to raise energy. The ritual recitation, usually rhymed, produces a magical effect. Although some feel that the words themselves contain power, it is usually the flow of the spoken words that elicits a reaction. However, since certain words often trigger magical thinking, the words themselves can play an important part.

Visualization is a technique that can be used throughout the magic working for various purposes. Energy can actually be raised using visualization. For example, while raising energy from within, one can visualize energy growing and perhaps being absorbed from the earth or sun.

Emotions are powerful forces that can be used by some as a means to raise energy. Anger especially is quite potent, but any emotion can be used. The basic idea is to link that emotion to the need of the working, such as directing anger towards a bad habit that one wishes to break. Since not everyone is comfortable working with his or her emotions in this way, this technique will not work with everyone. This technique can also be quite cathartic.

Just as music can be used to relax and even empower us while preparing for magic workings, it can also rouse our energy and help build it to higher levels. As the music increases in intensity, so does the energy we are raising, assuming that the practitioner has chosen music that has been found to be personally affective. In fact, an entire ritual could actually be centered on music alone if the practitioner is easily moved by music.

In many forms of magic, such as ceremonial magic, the evocation and invocation of spirits and other non-physical entities is used as a means of raising energy. Although often considered the same, technically, evocation is the summoning of an entity in a commanding way, whereas invocation is the act of conjuring such entities, often by their name, to petition them for help. Wiccans, for example, would invoke the deities and the powers of the quarters, welcoming them and asking for their assistance. Most Wiccans would not *evoke* them because, as a religion, reverence for these forces is a priority.

Evocations and *invocations*, especially in ceremonial magic, often make use of *sigils*. A sigil is an image that symbolizes a specific supernatural being (i.e. angel, demon, or spirit), and is used to summon the entity which it represents. They serve as visible signs for the invisible and are sometimes considered to have power over the evoked entity. Similarly, the *vévés* in Voodoo are intricate symbolic emblems drawn on the ground, often with flour, to invoke the various *loas* (ancestors or spirits) that they represent as well as serve as an altar for offerings.

As with the summoning of outside entities, certain physical objects such as amulets, talismans and charms can be used as a means of raising energy. There is actually a distinction between them that is often overlooked.

An amulet is usually a natural object that has been consecrated and possibly inscribed with magical symbols. Amulets are believed to possess power to protect a person physically and psychically from threatening influences and have power in and of themselves to work on behalf of the individual.

A talisman is a manmade object that has been charged with very specific properties, such as for fertility or good luck. It is often more specific in its purpose than an amulet. Talismans are usually charged with power by being inscribed and consecrated. The act of inscribing a talisman personalizes it and gives it purpose. Since they are believed to confer power on the individual, talismans are often used in magic work, focusing and adding to the power being raised.

Charms, which were originally considered to be the chanting of a verse to exert a magical influence over someone or something, is now often considered to be an object with combined properties of an amulet and talisman.

Like amulets, certain natural objects are often believed to contain energy or magical properties of their own. Herbs, trees, oils, and crystals are often used as natural amulets. Rose quartz, for example, is believed to be "in tune" with love and friendship and thus could add to the potency of a love spell. Similarly, the phases of the moon can be taken advantage of to enhance magic work. However, these things are not intended to be used as the actual means to achieve the objective, but rather as tools. In other words, running around with a chunk of rose quartz during the waxing moon in hopes of finding love is useless without the individual applying energy and direction toward the objective. Unfortunately, many "New Age" adherents seem to focus more on these tools than the actual application.

Natural rhythms such as phases of the moon, tides, seasons, astrological events, and for some, even days of the week can be used as subtle, but effective, additions to magic working. These rhythms not only have certain "flavors" of energy, but often have coinciding psychological effects that increase the resulting effectiveness of the work. Typically waning rhythms are useful for magic concerning such things as destruction and banishing (which includes the breaking of bad habits), wisdom, and divination, while the waxing rhythms are useful for magic concerning such things as healing, money, and growth.

STEP 3: DIRECTING ENERGY

Visualization is probably the most frequently used means of directing energy and will often be used in conjunction with the other methods listed below. By visualizing the flow of energy or the desired result, the raised energy is given momentum and direction. Since magic is very unpredictable, it is not recommended to visualize how something should occur, but simply what the final result should be.

There is also a psychological factor of visualization that should not be overlooked. Many researchers have shown that one is more likely to achieve a goal if it is first visualized. This, however, does not discount magic as being a purely psychological phenomenon, but rather shows the multiple levels on which the process of magic works.

Magic *does* include certain psychological features, and it does the practitioner well to pinpoint and utilize them. As mentioned in the section *Essence of Being*, the spiritual and physical aspects of our Being are joined by the intellectual aspect. This is the aspect where psychology is rooted.

Similar to visualization, symbols or objects that represent the goal or recipient can be used as a focal point in the directing of energy. In these cases, the practitioner is aware that these are representations not the destination of the directed energy.

Breathing is a very useful technique for controlling the flow of energy and helps to manifest this energy by providing a link on a physical plane. Exhaling is used to push out energy while inhaling is used to pull in energy.

As with breathing, physical gestures provide a physical link for the directing of energy. These gestures can be as simple as using the stronger hand (right for right-handed people, left for left-handed) for directing energy and the other hand for absorbing energy, to complex gestures such as tracing of invoking and banishing pentagrams. *(See Appendix A)*

Typically, these techniques are used in conjunction with others naturally. For example, a right-handed person may direct energy through the right hand while exhaling and visualizing that energy flowing out of the hand to the specific goal. Ideally, these techniques become second nature to the practitioner allowing for greater concentration on the desired result.

STEP 4: GROUNDING AND CENTERING

This step brings closure to the magic work as well as dissipates any remaining energy.

If external forms of energy were raised, such as with invocations and evocations, those energies need to be released, or "banished", in an appropriate manner. Although such energies will naturally dissipate in time, it is considered impolite – as well as unwise – to not formally banish that which was summoned. As with leaving an open flame unattended, there is always the possibility of undesired situations arising while these energies are still present.

Once this has been accomplished, the working space can be closed, if needed. If a circle was formally opened, it should be closed in a similar manner, if only to maintain a certain amount of discipline. Since external forms of energy should have already been released, and the next step would be for all individuals involved to ground any excess internal energy, the actual closing of the space could be seen as a mere formality. However, since many feel that the circle or workspace can be used as a means of containing energy, it is good practice to at least acknowledge that the space is no longer being used for magic.

Finally all individuals who were involved in the work must release personal (i.e. internal) energy (called grounding) and return to a level of consciousness better equipped for the mundane (called centering). Skipping this step leaves the practitioner in a "spacey" condition, which although not harmful or permanent, can be quite disconcerting.

Grounding and centering often go hand in hand and many techniques meet both needs at once. A very common technique is the consumption of food and beverages. This is often incorporated into the ritual structure such as the "Cakes and Ale" (or cookies and juice) portion of a Wiccan ritual. The consumption of food and drink helps focus the mind back on the physical. It is suggested that alcohol be avoided in excess since the affects of the alcohol would not be conducive to centering. Fruit juice is often used as a substitute. It is also a good idea to keep the intake in moderation while the body and mind return to a more grounded state to avoid nausea or hiccups.

Physical contact is another form of grounding, often in the form of touching the ground or a tree (when outdoors). Also touching one's face, hugging fellow members of a group, or simply stretching can aid in returning to a more physical perspective.

Some find that a form of visualization and/or meditation works well when grounding and centering. As discussed earlier, there is a strong link between visualization and the flow of energy. By visualizing surplus energy returning to the ground, we can actually dissipate it. Also, using the same techniques used to end meditation, one can ease the body and mind back to the physical.

Magic does not end with the spell or ritual. On the contrary, it has just begun. As discussed in the section entitled *Law of Action* in the previous chapter, magic is useless if the practitioner is not willing to make an effort to achieve the desired goal. If a spell is cast to find a job, then the practitioner must then be willing to follow leads as they become available and be willing to take risks if necessary. (Not to mention *look* for a job!) The act of working magic is an empowering tool: it acknowledges one's need and focuses one's will and intentions on that goal. To sit back and not take advantage of this negates the purpose of the magic working. Magic is not intended as an alternative to effort, but as a supplement to it.

APPLYING THE PRINCIPLES

Now that we have an idea of the structure of magic, we need to find practical applications. This is where the common idea of *know thyself* becomes apparent. Although magic has a simple structure, each step contains various means of performing them. The individual will find some things more effective than others, so experimentation and adaptation is essential.

The effectiveness of magic lies not in the procedure, but in how those procedures affect the practitioner. It is not enough to follow a spell or ritual verbatim as it is to use the structure of that spell or ritual effectively.

It astounds me how many people write me asking for "dark spells" as if the mere recitation of a spell has the power necessary to affect a change in the universe. The only use I have for the spell books I collect is in artistic appreciation. Sometimes these spells give me ideas for my own spells and rituals, but typically I read them merely for the pleasure of reading a type of poetry. A spell *is* a poem in that it should reach inward to the individual with its symbolism and touch one's heart and soul. When a spell has personal meaning in this manner, if it gives you goosebumps or makes you pause in silent reflection of its words, that spell has the potential for being effective in magic working.

The structure of certain traditional forms of magic may work well for some, but it would be a sad miscalculation to say that one form of magic is more effective or powerful than another. Certain systems will utilize techniques that may be more effective to some individuals over others.

It was my intent to provide an understanding of the underlying principles of magic while not dictating specific spells or rituals. Simply following someone else's spells from a book is too mechanical. It lacks depth. Such books may list the physical structure of the spell – what to say and do – but it does not explain how to raise and direct actual energy.

The dressing of candles, for example, is meaningless unless the practitioner uses this technique properly. Several principles are at work. The oil itself may be a natural source of external energy (for example rose oil is associated with love) which can subtly add to the energy being raised, while the scent provides an often powerful unconscious cue. The slow and repetitive act of dressing a candle not only assists in altering one's consciousness, but also provides a physical cue to the directing of energy into the candle and thus the magic itself. After all, the entire reason for dressing a candle for candle magic is to direct energy into it. Although this technique is often reserved for forms of candle magic, dressing the altar candles can be a useful means of ritual preparation as well.

Magic itself is a subtle art. Although natural objects and rhythms in and of themselves are not enough to work magic, they offer subtle, but often very distinctive, forms of energy. They are tools that can increase performance, but can not be relied on alone. True magic always starts and ends from within the practitioner.

The structure of a spell or ritual should be designed according to the needs of the practitioner, and not dictated by tradition or authority. A seasoned practitioner would use the techniques that are personally the most effective. This means that the practitioner should be able to dissect existing spells to locate the various techniques and, when necessary, replace them with techniques that would prove more effective for that individual.

Chaos Magic and Eclecticism

Chaos Magic and Dark Paganism are not the same, although many Dark Pagans no doubt find it intriguing and effective. Although not necessarily associated with Dark Paganism, Chaos Magic is more likely to be found on a dark path than a light path for the simple reason that it is more internal and dependant upon the practitioner and often goes against more traditional systems.

Trying to define Chaos Magic is no small task. Its very nature is so unstructured that to define it would take away its very essence.

Simply put, Chaos Magic is a magical "system" where truth is meaningless. No belief system is required and any belief system can be drawn from. In theory one could make something up and still find it just as effective as an ancient rite of a secret society.

This may seem very similar to eclectic magic. Both the chaotic magician and the eclectic magician would draw upon various, often unrelated, sources to perform magic or personalize a belief system. The eclectic however, attempts to build some sort of structure or system around these beliefs, whereas the chaotic magician is more concerned about using these beliefs as tools.

There is also a difference in attitude between the two. The eclectic magician attempts to find the truth behind the various sources and combine them to form a viable system. It is believed that these personalized systems, as well as the various systems from which the beliefs were drawn, share a common, intrinsic, or absolute truth that reaches beyond any given system.

The chaotic magician could not care less about such truths because it is believed there is no absolute truth: anything can be true just as it can be false. It is the magician who gives these beliefs their power, not the beliefs themselves. So while the beliefs of any given chaotic magician may be considered eclectic, the approach is quite different.

One of the advantages of Chaos Magic is that it can make use of powerful, yet fictitious imagery such as the archetypal characters called *The Endless* (including Dream, Desire, Death, and Destiny) of Neil Gaiman's graphic novels or the plethora of powerful magical imagery of the Dungeons and Dragons-based games.

Practitioners of Chaos Magic may seem on the surface to be disrespectful in their flagrant use of various beliefs – that they are simply trying to find an easy way past the more traditional forms of occult learning. Granted, many such people are attracted to it because of this impression, just as many are attracted to Dark Paganism because we are not afraid to accept that we desire a sense of power in our lives. However, such shallow people soon grow weary as they learn that their so thought "easy way" demands more than they were willing to give. The truth is, the chaotic magician must take it upon him/herself to empower the work being done. While most other practitioners have specific traditions or systems to draw upon, the chaotic magician must rely on him/herself to draw such connections to – and empower – the system or systems currently being used. This is not easily accomplished and requires great strength of will.

In the end, Chaos Magic is not for everyone. Some will find it of value while others, needing a more stable system, will prefer to stick with the more traditional approaches.

Basic Sex Magic

As I mentioned in my notes on raising energy, the power of an orgasm has throughout history been used for magical purposes. Unfortunately, this technique is often abused. This chapter discuses some of the basic principles of Western sex magic purely from a magical standpoint. Other Western forms of sex magic, such as Karezza, include religious and spiritual connotations that one may wish to explore further. Eastern practices such as Tantra are much too complex to cover in one chapter and require a religious and cultural connection in order to properly understand the terminology and principles at work. Spiritual-based sexual practices differ from purely magical-based sexual practices in that orgasm in spiritual-based sexual practice is often abstained by some or all involved. Magical-based practices typically harness the power of the orgasm itself.

Sex magic can be performed alone through masturbation, or with a partner or partners, although working with a partner increases the potential for complications.

In essence the sex act is used as a means to raise and direct energy produced during orgasm. The actual means of achieving an orgasm is inconsequential, although some prefer to ritualize the entire act. At a certain point, as an orgasm begins to build, the practitioner must begin to focus the energy and, at the actual point of orgasm, the energy must be directed towards its goal. It is very important to release and direct the energy just as the orgasm begins because the sexual energy, especially for men, will dissipate quickly.

The best way to direct energy in such a short window is to try to visualize the end result and hold that image during the orgasm as long as possible. You won't have time for animated visualization and you should plan in advance what this image will be. At the point of orgasm just concentrate as intensely as possible on the image. Some find that the image will seem to pulsate with each wave of orgasm, that is fine, but try to keep the image in focus for as long as possible. Visualization can also be used to envision the energy as it builds.

It is usually a good idea to hold an orgasm until it reaches a certain saturation point. Most sex manuals point out that the temporary stopping of genital stimulation a few times prior to the breaking stage of orgasm (i.e. the "point of no return") helps to increase the strength of the orgasm. Likewise, slow, flowing movements prolong the sex act, allowing the energy to build. This would not only increase pleasure, but the intensity of the orgasm, and thus the intensity of the energy being raised. Of course, magic working is not the time to experiment with new techniques so practice any new ideas before trying them in magic.

Breath control can also be used to enhance orgasm and control the flow of energy. Apart from its typical use in creating an altered state of consciousness, holding one's breath just prior to orgasm can increase its potency. Likewise, energy can be directed through exhaling as orgasm nears completion. Timing is important so it helps to truly observe one's orgasm during usual masturbation that is not part of magical practice. Few people really pay attention to what is happening to the body during orgasm since they are lost in the moment. Consciously observing an orgasm can lead to a better understanding of one's body and thus more effective use of one's orgasm.

Practicing sex magic requires a certain amount of maturity and strength of will since our natural instinct is to relax and enjoy the orgasm instead of attempting to harness its power. One also must overcome any feelings of shame or guilt that have been imposed upon sex and masturbation in most societies to perform this type of magic effectively.

Working with a partner or group has the benefit of adding each other's energy to the same goal, but does not come without a price. As with any group working, it is important to maintain a certain group mentality. If someone is not applying him/herself or is not in the right frame of mind, the focus of the entire group can be thrown off balance. Adding sex to this mix can obviously make this balance more volatile.

Often sex magic is used as an excuse for sex. Such abuses will destroy any chance of a successful working since the proper intent will not be present. It is very important to screen out such abusers, as well as reevaluate your own reasons for working with a partner or group.

Emotions can also cause complications in group workings. Feelings can easily be hurt and intentions may not be where they should. This can also cause complications after the magic working because some people equate sex with love. As romantic as this may seem at the time, experience teaches us this is simply not always the case. It is very important that those participating with a partner or partners in sex magic *clearly* understand what is being done and why. Although the partners do not necessarily have to be in a loving relationship to work together, it is a good idea for them to at least know each other and feel comfortable connecting with each other on such an intimate level. For this reason, most will find it better to work alone or only with one's lover. Either way, ALL partners need to be focused on the work at hand – raising and directing energy.

Any ethical issues or concerns for not being in a relationship with the partner need to be worked out long before working sex magic. The practitioners must be free of worry in order to concentrate on the work at hand.

Gender is another issue that needs to be addressed when working with a partner both in sex magic or any magic working. However, it is only an issue for those who find an issue with it. Some prefer to work in male/female pairs in order to work with traditional concepts of polarity. Granted, the energies of men and women differ in characteristic, and this difference could be taken advantage of in certain ways, but the *potency* of either will always depend on the *individual*, not the gender. As long as the partners are comfortable working with each other, gender and sexual preference have no bearing. We each contain both masculine and feminine energies, which is also why the use of a partner is optional.

The risks of pregnancy and sexually transmitted diseases are also very important concerns. Not only must these items be addressed for the welfare of the individuals, but these concerns could lurk in the back of one's mind, thus affecting concentration. There are actually some that insist that pregnancy will not occur if the magic is done correctly. This is absolutely absurd. It is the responsibility of all involved to ensure the safety of the group. The use of contraception will *not* adversely effect the outcome of the magic, assuming it does not prevent orgasm. If the partners agree to not use contraception then they must be willing to take responsibility for the results, unwanted pregnancy being the least of the risks.

Since it is virtually impossible for a group of people to achieve orgasm at the same time, let alone a couple, some sort of protocol needs to be established among the participants. Those who have already achieved orgasm and spent a few moments resting can direct energy towards the partner who is preparing for orgasm. This is assuming that the partners have already made some sort of agreement that they both wish to achieve orgasm. Some couples may find it more affective to focus on the first person to orgasm and then stop. This is something that needs to be discussed well before the actual working and agreed upon by all participants.

As with other forms of magic the structure of the magic work and flow of consciousness defined in the chapter *The Structure of Magic* remains the same. Sex magic is simply one technique among many in the working of magic. Taken seriously, sex magic can be an extremely potent tool.

Characteristics of the Practitioner

I was originally going to skip this chapter completely since I did not want to appear dogmatic or in any way involve ethics. However, keeping these concerns aside, there are some characteristics that any practitioner of magic, or for that matter any individual exploring one's spirituality, would find useful to keep in mind. Most of these characteristics will seem common sense, although it is usually the most obvious that we so often miss.

Patience

Magic is not for the impatient or those who easily give up. Immediate results should not be expected. Many beginners become too easily discouraged over a short period of study/training. This is more often than not because the expectations of magic supersede the reality of what magic truly encompasses. We are also accustomed, in modern society, to immediate

results.   There are some things in life that
technology cannot speed up.   Learning is a slow
process that should not be rushed.   It consists of
more than simply memorization, but also
experimentation and even failure.   It is a *growing*
process and never truly ends.

Confidence

Magic is not an exact science.   We do not yet
understand the forces that are being tapped, nor
do we fully understand how to access and direct
these forces.   In a sense, the magical practitioner
of today is a pioneer into an unknown aspect of
nature.   Perhaps science will one day allow us to
comprehend the true nature of these forces and
magic, science, and spirituality will once again
combine.   Until then we must experiment with the
little we truly know and explore this new frontier,
often alone.

Before there can be success, there is often failure.
We have probably heard this cliché many times. A
good practitioner must build a sense of confidence
in order to see beyond the failures of the present
and not give up.   Failures are the building blocks
of success and are only a loss when we fail to
learn from them.

Doubts and fears of failure will only hinder one's
concentration and effectiveness.   Man's greatest
enemy is himself. *We are what we think.* In many
ways, we create our own reality.   How we perceive
ourselves is what determines who we are and how
we present ourselves to others.

Confidence also allows us to not be hindered by concerns of joining a coven or reaching certain degrees of initiation. Although some may find group work beneficial, others will find it very restricting. One does not *need* to be initiated by a tradition in order to be an effective practitioner. Many collect initiations like medals, hoping they will finally feel accepted. This acceptance, of course, will never happen since such people have never accepted *themselves*. True initiation is an *internal* process – not an external ritualized process. An initiation ritual symbolizes the internal changes that the initiate has undergone, although the actual ritual may have profound meaning to an initiate because of those internal changes.

Skepticism

Skepticism can be a useful trait assuming it is not actually a lack of self-confidence in disguise. The skeptic does not accept anything at face value and seeks to find the truth for him/herself.

Memorizing texts simply because they are popular works does nothing for the practitioner if he or she cannot find practical applications through experimentation. These texts are merely empty words until the practitioner finds meaning from within. Tables of correspondences for herbs, trees, colors, quarters, etc. are useful starting points but must have internal meaning to the practitioner to be empowered. These things should never be taken as strict, unyielding associations.

Desire

Desire is a driving force of humanity. There is nothing wrong with the desire to obtain power and material wealth, although these things in excess have the potential to cause one to stagnate. If it were possible to obtain all our desires we would no longer strive for anything and would eventually tire of life. It is desire itself that motivates us and gives life momentum. Fortunately, we are inherently insatiable creatures and so it is very unlikely that we could ever reach such a state.

Although desire is often shunned by those who feel it is a vice, it is the way that desires are obtained that is of issue. However, this is where ethics becomes involved and that is not the scope of this chapter. Needless to say, desire in and of itself is nothing to be ashamed about.

From time to time it is useful to write down a list of all your desires in order to better discover and reach your goals. It is surprising how often we really do not know what we desire. For example, I often say I desire money, but on reflection of *why* I want that money I see that it is to satisfy other deeply-rooted desires such as to have more free time for my spiritual pursuits and writing, or to be able to explore the world without having to worry about bills and other financial obligations that hold me down. My desire, as it turns out, was not the money itself but what I hoped to obtain with that money. I also discovered that I could do other things to obtain some of these goals, such as learning better time management. By concentrating on my assumption that money was the only way, I spent more of my free time trying to make money and thus I was left with even less free time to do the things I truly wanted.

Desire is only a motivational force when we can realize the actual *goal*. Often there is more than one way to achieve our goals, but we will not see those alternate paths until we step back and look at the "big picture" without the bias of our perception of the ideal means to that goal.

A Word of Warning

Within all of us is a sadist, a predator, even a killer. For some this is more so than others, but no one is free of a dark side. Delving into one's shadow-self, opening the floodgates, exacts its toll. It may be a tremendous feeling of shame or depression, or waves of fear. It may stir up a violent side that was imprisoned by a wall of denial. Past trauma long thought resolved or forgotten may return to the surface. For some this may be more than was expected and possibly more than can be handled.

Should you find yourself in this situation, you are not alone. It is very advantageous to have the availability of a close friend while dealing with the dark recesses of one's unconscious to provide a reference to the external world. Such a person can be an anchor to reality and be a source of reinforcement when such dark realizations overwhelm us with a sense of unworthiness or inferiority.

Do not be afraid to seek professional help through a qualified therapist. This is not a sign of weakness. It simply means you are being overwhelmed with the feelings that were released and need help sorting them all out. You are the best judge in determining what you can handle and what you cannot. Trust your instinct and put pride aside. Confrontation with one's dark side is a humbling experience to say the least.

The path to one's soul may be a solitary one, but one must know when to use the tools at one's disposal and that includes the use of friends or professionals. Therapy can be a powerful tool if taken seriously by both the client and the therapist. It may take time to find the right person for the task, but the effort is well worth it.

Don't take this lightly. Those with strong, possibly unrealized neuroses or psychoses may find exploration into their dark side dangerous. If you already know you are unstable and still have the urge to enter the shadows, do so with the aid of a professional – ideally one with Jungian influences.

Am I going Insane?

If you need to ask, then chances are you are working through the problem and have no need to fear. We all have our share of complexes and neuroses that can adversely effect our behavior, yet still we maintain a strong enough grasp on reality to be considered "normal." In fact it *is* normal to have such aberrations – within reason. However, sometimes those attracted to themes of darkness are motivated by borderline mental illness. This chapter is in no way a substitute for obtaining professional help, but can be useful to stable individuals who have come across an emotional or psychological stumbling block along the way.

Dealing with Depression

When working with one's shadow, depression is bound to arise. It is a natural and healthy phase of individuation – the process of becoming a whole and unique individual. Depression clouds our perception, focusing all attention and negative emotions inward. At the time it will seem as if such a condition is unlikely to pass. However, it *will* pass, and we can handle more than we give ourselves credit for.

Becoming aware of negative or embarrassing traits we did not even know we had is a very disconcerting experience. The nature of these traits are often completely in opposition to what we hold to be our true Selves. However, given time and understanding, the ego eventually sorts out the internal conflict and expands upon the sense of self. Once this happens, depression lifts and the psychic energy we have been unconsciously using to suppress those uncovered aspects of ourselves becomes available for us to deepen or widen our consciousness.

So when depression seems to be suffocating you, try to work out those feelings – find a way to express them. Cry, talk to a trusted friend or family member, write about it in a journal, express it in art or dance. The more you consciously attempt to deal with the conflict, the sooner your ego will be able to heal and grow. Don't wallow in your own self-pity for too long – what good does that do you?

Finally, take responsibility for your feelings. Instead of finding fault with the world, find the fault in yourself and cope with it. Instead of placing the blame for your emotional pain on others, accept that you and you alone are the cause of that pain. Your perceptions stem from within, as does the pain that follows. Once this is understood, we are given back the control of our own lives that we have thrown onto others. Yes, this sucks, but it is not impossible. No one ever said the path to self-understanding was an easy one!

Should you find yourself thinking more and more of suicide, then you know you have gone too far too soon and need to stop and call someone. Don't wait until later – seek help right now. Call your operator and ask to be connected to a helpline, or consult your area phonebook for some organizations that can help. Humans have the innate ability to survive through great hardships, even when it seems impossible. Eventually we adapt to the situation or find ways to adapt the situation to us – it is our nature. Suicide is a weak-minded way to escape suffering and serves no legitimate or viable purpose.

Mystical Experience or Psychosis?

There has long been a debate over the significance in the relationship between psychosis and a mystical (or religious) experience. The findings, of course, vary and are of little importance to this book as a whole. However, since a mystical experience can be quite powerful and transformative, and since working with darker imagery and archetypes can increase the chance of releasing already-existing but semi-dormant psychoses, these topics are worthy of exploration.

What is a Mystical Experience?

A mystical experience is not something that can be fully defined since our normal state of consciousness has no frame of reference on which to grasp such an experience in its entirety. Regardless of our religious beliefs, our usual perception of our environment functions within a dualism of "the Self" and "Others." We perceive these as being separate, regardless of the possibility of an absolute underlying wholeness, because our perception is based on the perspective of our ego. During a mystical experience, this dualism, and thus our ego, is transcended and we sense this wholeness of the universe as an absolute truth. As this experience closes, we naturally interpret it through our personal ideology. Therefore, those with a specific religious ideology would interpret the experience as a religious experience.

The experience itself, be it interpreted as religious or not, is very powerful. The individual will be overcome with a sense of joy or wonder. While such experiences can range from mild to intense, the more intense experiences can be so emotionally overwhelming that it can completely alter one's lifestyle or perception. Overall, the experience is considered positive and can result in improvements in the individual's functionality.

What is Psychosis?

A psychosis is characterized by a loss of contact with reality and is generally taken in a negative context. Unlike a neurosis, where the individual is aware that he or she has a problem, a psychotic does not realize that his or her behavior and perceptions have no basis in reality. Psychosis is what one would commonly term "madness."

Some psychotic episodes are brief and may never return. We have all experienced a minor form of this when overcome by an emotion such as rage or grief where we have said or done things we would not normally do. Sometimes, certain factors in our lives such as stress bring us to our breaking point where we are no longer able to cope with the issues. These, "mental breakdowns", as they are called – although frightening – are usually recoverable.

More severe or chronic forms of psychosis steer us too far away from reality and require professional assistance and possibly medication to bring about some form of recovery or stability. Such episodes typically include hallucinations and drastic prolonged changes in our behavior.

Mystical vs. Psychotic

Many who suffer from psychotic episodes, such as in the case of schizophrenia, may interpret the experience as a mystical experience. Outwardly it may be hard to distinguish the descriptions of the experiences from that of the legitimately mystical, but the effects the experience has on the individual is often where the separation can be made.

Both are disruptions of normal consciousness but their effects on us are very different. After a mystical experience there is a sense of sacredness and holiness. The experience itself is meaningful and has beneficial effects on one's outlook on life. Those who hallucinate divine communication during a psychotic episode do not have the same profound positive results as a true mystical experience. Such hallucinations are often followed by a sense of no longer being human or mortal, or result in terror or increased paranoia.

Keep in mind that the most creative individuals are often perceived as being a bit strange. Creativity itself relies on a change in perception of reality and a greater connection to one's unconscious. A certain loosening of one's grip on reality allows for new and powerful perspectives, but also can be seen as a prelude to psychosis. The line between insanity and genius is a fine one and far from complete.

Possessions and Hauntings

As discussed in the chapter *On "Demons" and "Evil Spirits"*, although the possibility for such malicious entities exists, the danger is more often from within. To understand this it helps to first understand the nature of a complex.

Complexes are emotionally charged groups of ideas or images with which we in some way were unable to effectively cope. We all have complexes – they express the issues and problems we wrestle with internally and thus mark our vulnerabilities. Existing as their own self-contained construct in the mind, complexes seem to have a voice of their own. They may be the nagging voice of our father telling us not to show weakness or a teacher telling us we will never amount to anything. Coupled with the power of repression and the shadow, complexes can seem to have a mind of their own within our consciousness, throwing out ideas that seem foreign to our ego. It is not surprising that people thought this to be the work of demons during the Middle Ages.

Of course, a subtle sense of the presence of an outside influence is one thing, but the actual perception of physical manifestations is another. Keep in mind that hallucinations affect *all* the senses, not just sight. Food can taste bad and we can hear voices that seem to come from outside our heads. During such drastic experiences it is wise to seek input from others. Although on rare occasions an actual outside entity or force may be to blame, more often than not these are signs of psychosis and should be treated accordingly, which includes professional help.

Since the sufferer of a psychotic episode will not be able to determine the difference between a real threat and a *perceived* threat, there is little this book can do to assist. If possible, try to remain calm and focused and seek some guidance from someone you can trust. Typically a banishing ritual will improve the situation in the case if a true outside threat. Such encounters are rarely dramatic so this is often a quick way to separate reality from potential hallucination.

Needless to say, if you are already on medication for schizophrenia or other forms of psychosis, venturing into the realm of shadow work or magical practice is far from wise.

The topic of hauntings and possessions is discussed from a metaphysical perspective in *Appendix B* of this book.

What will Others Think?

In the process of individuation, we seek to become aware of, and sometimes incorporate, aspects of ourselves that we have long repressed into the shadow. Often the reason for the repression in the first place was so that we could better fit into society. Conforming allows for a greater acceptance by our peers. It does not take long to discover this when we start school, and it remains with us long after graduation into the workplace: the less you stand out the fewer waves you make and thus the more comfortably you live... or so it seems at least.

How much of our energy is spent trying to adapt and conform to the norms of society? How much can we truly know of our selves if we are too busy trying to measure up to external expectations? We are trained from birth to become slaves of "what people do" and "what people think." What happens to that unique spark that defines who you really are? It becomes buried under so much emotional baggage and social responsibility that we dare not attempt to look back. And so we live our lives, find a job, get married, have 2.5 kids, a car, and a house with a white picket fence because that is how we were *told* to be happy. Then, in the fury of midlife crisis we wonder what happened to our youth and dreams.

Are you happy? Are you who you want to be? Chances are, if you are reading this book, at one time something within you said "no." The reason why those who walk a dark path don't always "fit in" is because they choose to follow their *own* path, their *own* principles. They search for their *own* truth and not that which has been force-fed to them since birth. Ask yourself what it is it about darkness that fascinates you; chances are that it is the rebellious images of those aligned with darkness, or the very concept of its internal nature that attracts you – those voices within you calling you home.

To realize your wholeness, you must free yourself from the power that the collective mind has over you. You must break free from the fear of looking stupid or useless and focus on finding your own path, your own ways. What will the world think of you? Who cares!

A Final Word

Eventually the New Age movement will attempt to water down the material presented in this book to make it more palatable to the masses. It will no doubt seem more forgiving and comforting, but heed my words: No matter how watered down the presentation, the results cannot be softened or controlled. One's dark side cannot be destroyed by "healing light" – that is simply a visualization technique for repression and causes more harm than good in the long run. ***This is not a journey to be taken lightly!*** Call out to the darkness long enough and eventually you WILL get an answer. If you are not willing to face such consequences, then stick to safer practices.

Our dark side is a permanent part of us that must be accepted for us to grow. Some of it has no use other than to point out that we are not angels. Other aspects can be harnessed to bring us balance. In the shadows, the passionless find lust, which can lead to passion if embraced. The underdog finds a voice. The prey finds aggression. Overall we become more whole.

This is not a path for everyone: for some the price may seem too high. The weak-minded, the ignorant, the self-delusioned, they will be the first to crumble and the first to condemn these ideas. For those who accept the challenge, the path into the shadows holds the key to unlocking our hidden potential and truly understanding who we are. We may not always like what we see, but when stripped of all the trappings of ego we have the power to truly choose how we live our lives.

Damnant Quod Non Intelligunt
("They Condemn What They Do Not Understand")

Appendix A: Invoking/Banishing Pentagrams

The invoking and banishing pentagrams are the tracings of a pentagram in the air in a specific way as a gesture of opening/beginning and closing/ending, respectively. This is usually done with either an athame or the index and pointing fingers of the stronger hand (the hand you write with).

These gestures are used at various points in a ritual including the calling and banishing of the quarters, the blessings of objects, the sealing of spells, or the temporary opening/closing of a circle once it has been cast. The use, if used at all, will depend on the individual or tradition.

As always, the power lies not in the symbol or gesture, but in the practitioner. Ritual gestures merely assist the practitioner in maintaining the proper mental context needed for ritual. They are simply an outer form of what is happening internally.

There are countless variations of invoking and banishing pentagrams, so only one common form will be outlined in this appendix. Sometimes these pentagrams are sealed with a circle traced in a deosil (clock-wise) direction.

Invoking Pentagram

The invoking pentagram is used to symbolize a beginning or opening as well as in blessings.

Starting at the top point, work down to the bottom left point, then diagonally up across to the right. Continue in one sweeping motion the rest of the pentagram. It will end back where the tracing began at the top point. (If you were doing this with a pencil, the pencil would never leave the paper during the tracing.)

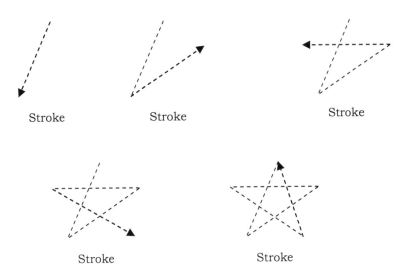

Stroke   Stroke   Stroke

Stroke   Stroke

Banishing Pentagram

The banishing pentagram is used to symbolize a closing or ending as well as the sealing of a spell. Like the invoking pentagram, it should be traced in one sweeping motion starting and ending at the lower left.

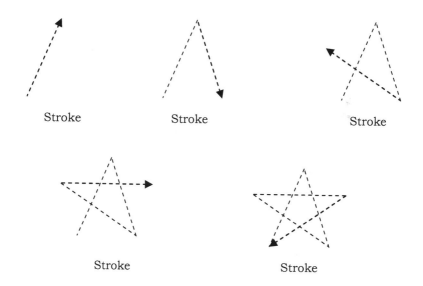

Stroke Stroke Stroke

Stroke Stroke

Appendix B: Hauntings and Possessions Revisited

As mentioned in the chapter on Essence of Being, we are composed of three aspects: Physical ("body"), Mental ("mind") and Spiritual ("soul/spirit"). Our identity as Self is based on the interaction and intersection of these three levels or aspects of our Being – all three are necessary to give us identity.

At the moment of death, our body ceases to function on its own – however, this in itself does not define death: a body can be kept functioning through the use of various machines while the mind is long gone. Death, as it so happens, is defined when the brain ceases to function and cannot be revived; when someone is "brain dead" they are considered past the point of return. Metaphysically, brain death is when the body, our physical aspect, loses its capacity to connect and interact with the mental aspect – that which bridges us to the spiritual and allows us to function on the physical plane.

Once this connection is severed, we are "dead" and the connection between the mental and spiritual begins to deteriorate. Under normal circumstances, the mental aspect dissipates within an hour of death, lingering over the corpse like an invisible mist while the spiritual aspect completes its cycle, returning to its source. Some religions would go further to say this spiritual aspect is then reincarnated or moved to a new dimension of life, such as an afterlife, but the fact of the matter is, any discourse on what happens after death (including what is presented here) is purely speculation based on personal belief and insight.

Sometimes, when conditions are just right, the natural death process as described above is prolonged. When a person dies suddenly or violently, refuses to accept death, and/or has a strong will coupled with the need to accomplish a task, the consciousness latches onto the physical plane – typically through a place or object with a strong emotional association with that person. Emotions are powerful energy forms that are created and experienced by the internal interactions of all aspects of our being. Such emotional energy can temporarily sustain this "*remnant entity*" which consists of the loosely connected mental and spiritual aspects of the deceased's being.

When this remnant entity has a strong enough connection to the physical plane, it is perceived as a "ghost" by the living. Typically this perception is on an unconscious level which is why such entities are rarely seen, and when they are it is brief and subtle and the experience is often more of an emotional than a physical one.

Certain places that are natural "pools" of psychic energy have the ability to prolong the dissipation process of these remnant entities, although in all cases they gradually dissipate. This is why hauntings are typically of spirits less than 200 years old. Such places instill a sense of "silent attraction" or fascination even to the living, and thus are labeled "haunted" or "sacred" places depending on the way the energy is perceived.

Remnant entities, or ghosts, lack the ability of self-reflection and true identity since memory itself was stored in the physical construct of the brain which was left with the body at death. All that remains are some emotionally charged trace memories burned into the mental aspect at the time of death. These trace memories are usually of the cause of death or the dying wishes of the individual. Certain emotional traumas experienced during one's life can also leave traces on the mental aspect that could be equated to the scars of a severe physical wound. Without the ability of self-reflection, remnant entities are locked into reactionary patterns based on their limited perception.

Additionally, as the bond between the mental and spiritual aspect weakens, the mental aspect loses even more touch with its former identity until it is no longer perceived as the spirit of the deceased but rather as an inhuman entity. In such rare cases where a remnant entity has degraded to the point of losing its association to its former identity, but is still latching onto the physical, it becomes warped and confused. Such entities manifest as psychic disturbances such as poltergeists (external disturbances) or what is perceived as an "evil spirit" by many cultures (internal disturbances).

Involuntary spiritual possessions are rare phenomena more commonly caused by a degraded ("lost") remnant entity than an actual "demonic" entity. They occur when the natural psychic defenses of a person with a mind that is overly receptive to outside influences becomes very weak (typically from prolonged mental or physical illness). Such a person is likely to have little will to live or lack a strong or stable personality. A lost remnant entity still clinging to the physical plane is able to "plug in" to that person's consciousness. The ongoing struggle in the living person's consciousness is the manifestation of such a possession. Since the invading consciousness no longer has a clear identity, it associates itself with how it is perceived by the resident consciousness of the inflicted individual. Depending on the culture, the invading entity may associate itself as an evil spirit or demon, for example. They can also be perceived as a psychosis, although most psychoses are not related to an actual possession.

At this point in a possession, a psychic co-dependent relationship develops. The invading consciousness achieves some sense of awareness and identity (albeit warped) and the resident consciousness, which was often stagnating, is given momentum from the struggle, or the invasion itself fills an emptiness or psychic need.

Once established, the invading entity can only be exorcised if the resident consciousness wills it. This is why the exorcism rituals of various cultures are based on empowering the victim and instilling a sense of faith and self-worth. When such a state is reached, one's natural psychic defenses kick in and repel the invader. However, such rituals are not 100% effective because of the co-dependent nature of the individual. Addictions are never truly cured but can be controlled. One who has suffered a possession must face the same daily struggle as anyone else fighting an addiction, for until the invading entity has fully dissipated it will always share a psychic link to the victim.

One note on possessions: not all possessions are of this negative nature. Many tribal cultures summon their ancestor spirits and experience moments of spiritual possession during their rites. In these cases the practitioners willingly bring themselves to a condition conducive to possession by achieving a trance-like state and weakening the body by means of dance and/or fasting. These experiences are positive and strengthen the connection among the community and the ancestral spirits. The effectiveness of such rights is culturally dependent and a result of a strong faith and thus not likely to work for the merely curious.

Bibliography

I am sure there have been many more books that have influenced me during the course of writing this book and the essays from which it was derived. Below are books I specifically referenced while researching the Deities and the Shadow. Authors such as Starhawk and LaVey, although not listed here have no doubt influenced my spiritual development over the years and are strongly recommended.

Baumgartner, Anne S. *Ye Gods!*. Lyle Stuart Inc., Secaucus, NJ. 1984.

Branden, Nathaniel. *The Disowned Self.* Bantham Books, New York. 1978.

Brown, Joseph Epes. *The Spiritual Legacy of the American Indian.* Crossroad Publishing Company, new York. 1982.

Budge, E.A. Wallis. *Amulets and Talismans.* The Macmillian Company, New York. 1970.

_____. *The Egyptian Book of the Dead.* Dover Publications, Inc., New York. 1967.

Campbell, Joseph. *The Power of Myth.* Anchor Books/Doubleday, New York. 1988.

Camporesi, Piero. *Juice of Life*. Continuum, New York. 1995.

Cavendish, Richard, ed. *An Illustrated Encyclopedia of Mythology*. Orbis Publishing Ltd., London. 1980.

Homer. *The Odyssey of Homer.* University of California Press, Berkley, CA. 1990

Horsley, Edith M. & Hole, Christina. *The Encyclopedia of Superstitions.* Helicon Publishing Ltd. 1961.

Jung, Carl Gustav. *Collected Works, vols. 1-20.* Princeton University Press, Princeton, NJ. 1953-1990

_____. *Memories, Dreams Reflections.* Pantheon Books, New York. 1973.

_____. "The Fight with the Shadow". Listener, November 7, 1946.

_____. *Two Essays on Analytical Psychology.* Princeton University Press, Princeton, NJ. 1966.

Laguerre, Michel S., *Voodoo Heritage.* Sage Publications, London. 1980.

MacCana, Proinsias. *Celtic Mythology.* Hamlyn Publishing Group, London. 1970.

Welch, Holmes. *Taoism: The Parting of the Way.* Beacon Press, Boston. 1966.

Table of figures

Index

A

Adrasteia. *See Nemesis*
Alcohol, 210, 218
Amulets, 214
Ankh, 51
Anubis, 160
Archetypes, 48, 89
  Dark, 48
Ares, 170
Asatru, 120
Athena, 157
Aura, The, 184, 186

B

Badhbh. *See Morrigan, The*
Balance, 14, 133
Banishing, 217
Banishing Pentagram,
  216, 253
Bathing, Ritual, 205
BDSM, 34, 111
BDSM Subculture, 34
Between the Worlds, 202
Binding Spell, 91
Blood, 29, 109, 110
  Drinking, 28, 40
Blot, 121
Bones, 53
Bone-turning, 54
Breathing, 203, 216, 229
Burning Times, 71, 72,
  143

C

Cakes and Ale, 218
Calaveras, 54
Candles, Dressing, 220
Cemeteries, 49
Centering, 217
Cernunnos, 164
Chaos (deity), 167
Chaos Magic, 223

Characteristics of the
  Practitioner, 233
Charon, 160
Chi, 31, 139
Circumcision, 114
  Female, 115
  Male, 114
Clitoridectomy, 114
Collective Shadow, 70
Collective Unconscious, 48
Complex, 245
Concentration, 203
Confidence, 234
Conformity, 117, 247
Covens, 235
Crone, The, 153
Crossroads, 52
Crow, The, 53
Crows, 52, 156
Cupid. *See Eros*
Curse, 90

D

Dance, 205, 212
Dark Paganism, 11, 14,
  137
Dark Path, 95, 131, 132,
  134
Dark Spirituality, 123
Darkness, 11, 43, 46, 95
  Aspects of, 44
  Mystery and, 47
  Power and, 47, 95
  Seductiveness, 46
Darksiders, 19, 23, 33, 46,
  64
  Commonalities, 36
Day of the Dead. *See Dia
  de los Muertos*
Death, 46, 50, 136, 159,
  255
Deinos, 170
Deities, 151
  As Archetypes, 89

INDEX

I

Id, The, 66
Imagery, Dark, 48, 74
Incantation, 212
Individuation. *See*
    Shadow, The
Initiation, 128, 235
Intellectual Essence of
    Being, 190, 201
Intuition, 186
Invocation, 213
Invoking Pentagram, 216,
    252

J

Jung, Carl, 48, 55, 66
Justice as Archetype, 57

K

Kali, 167

L

LARP, 27
Left Hand Path. *See Dark*
    Path
Light Path, 131
Lightside Paganism, 15
Lightsiders, 64
Lilith, 171
Loas, 213
Loki, 173

M

Macha, 155
Mad Scientist as
    Archetype, 56
Mage as Archetype, 56
Magic, 178, 180, 197, 221
    Application of, 219
    Chaos. *See Chaos Magic*
    Eclectic. *See Eclectic*
        Magic

Limitations of, 180
Nature of, 177
Psychological factors of,
    181, 215, 216
Sex. *See Sex Magic*
Structure of, 197
Mars (god). *See Ares*
Martial Arts, 205
Meditation, 203
Mental Essence of Being.
    See Intellectual Essence
    of Being
Midlife Crisis, 74
Min, 166
Mind-altering Substances,
    208
Minerva. *See Athena*
Monism, 126
Monster as Archetype, 57
Moros, 168
Morpheus, 169
Morrigan, The, 156
Mors, 163
Music, 207, 213
Mystery, 47
Mystery Religion, 105
Mystical Experience, 242,
    243
Myth, 48

N

Natural Rhythms, 215
Nemesis (goddess), 167
Nemhain. *See Morrigan,*
    The
Neurosis, 244
New Age Movement, 45,
    64, 70, 133, 197, 215,
    248
Niflheim. *See Hel*
Night, The, 59
    Past Associations, 59
    Present Associations, 60
Nyx, 169

INDEX

INDEX

Printed in Great Britain
by Amazon